CW00801253

The Complete Breville Smart Air Fryer Oven Cookbook for Beginners

Quick, Easy and Delicious Recipes for Smart People on a Budget

Cora Paradiso

TABLE OF CONTENTS

INTRODUCTION

What Is Breville?

Breville is an Australian manufacturer of small home appliances (based in Sydney), including premium countertop ovens, non-premium ovens (like a regular toaster oven), blenders, microwaves, and also makes Nespresso coffee machines. The company was founded in 1932 and the brand name Breville was taken from the two founders' last names: Bill O'Brien and Harry Norville.

In 2002, the Breville brand was introduced to the United States and in recent years has introduced juicers, pressure cookers, food processors, and blenders. By 2011, sales for its juicers doubled by the U.S. following a Breville juicer featured in the Netflix series 'Fat, Sick and Nearly Dead.' The Breville Smart Oven is also one of the latest launches of Breville 's product.

THE BREVILLE SMART OVEN AIR

The Breville Smart Oven Air has many features similar to those of Breville's other, ovens or even a toaster oven. Breville countertops are renowned for having many features and functions. The Breville smart stainless steel oven has features that you would expect as a slow cook and baking feature plus a couple more including Air Fry and Dehydrate. Air frying is a healthier way to crunch your food than conventional frying oil. Air frying is using Super Convection 's intelligent machine to help move air inside the oven for the best crisp. Super Convection runs the built-in convection ventilator at speeds much higher than normal Convection cooking. The two-speed convection fan is one of the small-appliance market's only two-speed fans.

For every cooking function, the Element IQ device works to optimize the heating elements, convection fan, and time to achieve the best results for each task. For each mode, you can use the Element IQ program, or just manually use your oven.

The lowest-priced countertops in Breville are without convection fans. These are not convection ovens while the Breville Smart Oven Pro (the variant in price just below the Smart Air) has a convection fan but not a two-speed fan.

WHAT ARE THE SMART OVEN AIR FUNCTIONS?

The Smart Air has 13 preset features, that's quite a lot. The following functions are: Bake, Roast, Broil, Warm, Pizza, Proof, Air Fry, Toast, Bagel, Reheat, Slow Cook, Cookies and Dehydrating.

All of these preset functions works with the Element IQ System of the company and each of the six oven heating elements to cook automatically for optimal performance. These heating elements are placed on top and bottom of the oven, and each element is turned on or off by the Element IQ System at higher or lower power, depending on the feature you select.

HOW DO I USE MY BREVILLE AIR FRYER?

As described above, the Element IQ system uses the heating elements of the oven at higher or lower temperatures, and turns some on or off to cook the best way you choose. We 're explaining these modes here so you know what sorts of stuff your Breville air fryer can cook with.

Roast

Roast mode is intended for the cooking of thick meat or poultry cuts. Ideally, roasting adds a crisp exterior to what you cook while leaving moist and tender inside. Note that when using Roast, use rack position 6 in the oven (the location of the rack is indicated at the window of the oven to let you know where position 6 is located).

Bake

Bake mode is designed to use heat to cook cookies, muffins, and similar food evenly in the top and bottom of your oven. Baking also works well in your included baking pan or on the wire rack with dense savory frozen dishes such as lasagna or pot-pies. Using oven rack position 6 when using Bake mode, as in Roast mode, and use rack position indicator on the oven window to show where position 6 is located.

Broil

Broiling is about searing the top side of your food at high temperatures. Broil mode uses the heating elements at the top of the oven to crisp open-faced sandwiches, thinly sliced beef, seafood, sausages, and vegetables at their maximum power.

Toast

Toast is what you might anticipate, essentially cooking the bread's top layer while keeping the inside soft and moist. Toast mode can also be used to heat and crisp English muffins and frozen waffles. Use oven position 4 in Toast mode . The oven suits up to 9 slices of conventionally sliced bread. Using the "Time" dial in the control panel of the oven to pick the amount of slices you are toasting with.

Bagel

The Bagel mode is designed to cook the inside of a thick bagel, crumpet, or specialty bread and only toast the outside lightly. For Bagel mode, using rack position 4 (see the positions indicated on the window). The oven is designed to accommodate up to 10 slices of bagel.

BENEFITS OF BREVILLE SMART AIR FRYER OVEN

Here are some benefits:

- Every heating system automatically adjusts to match your preferred setting
- Super convection setting reduces cooking time by 30% while providing perfect crispness — ensuring quick and even roasting, frying and dehydration of the air
- The 13 pre-programmed settings include: toast, bagel, broil, bake, roast, hot, pizza, proof, air-frying, reheating, cookies, slow cooking and dehydration
- Six independent quartz heating elements transfer the power where food is most needed — above and below — resulting in an effective cooking process
- Air-frying function combines high heat and super-convection to maximize airflow, resulting in deliciously crispy food
- PID regulation eliminates over-shooting for accurate and stable temperatures
- Large-capacity countertop oven lets you roast a 14-lb. turkey, toast nine slices of bread, bake a 12-cup muffin tray...

Air Fryer Bacon

Prep Time: 2 minutes, Servings: 2

Ingredients

*   5 strips bacon

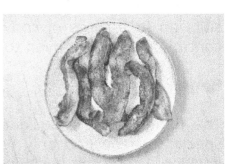

Instructions

*   Place the strips of bacon onto the air fryer rack.
*   Air fry the bacon at 375 degrees F for 10 minutes, flipping once if needed.
*   Once the bacon is fully cooked remove the bacon from the air fryer and place onto paper towels or whatever you use to absorb the bacon grease.

Nutrition Info

Calories: 229kcal, Protein: 6g, Fat: 21g, Saturated Fat: 7g, Cholesterol: 36mg, Sodium: 364mg, Potassium: 108mg, Iron: 0.2mg

Air Fryer-Perfectly Done, Heavenly French Toast

Prep/Cook Time: 11, 1 serving

Ingredients

*   4 slices of bread
*   2 eggs
*   2/3 cup of milk
*   1 teaspoon of vanilla
*   1/2 teaspoon of cinnamon

Instructions

*   In a small bowl mix together the eggs, milk, cinnamon, and vanilla. Then beat until the eggs are broken up and everything is mixed well.
*   Then dip each piece of bread into the mixture and then shake to get the excess off, as you do, put them into your prepared pan

- Air Fryer for 3 minutes at 320 degrees F. Then flip them over and do another 3 minutes.
- Serve with maple syrup and enjoy!

Nutrition Info

144 calories, 6g fat (1g saturated fat), 73mg cholesterol, 509mg sodium, 11g carbohydrate (3g sugars, 2g fiber), 15g protein.

Easy Air Fryer Broccoli

Prep/Cook Time: 15 mins, Servings: 2 servings

Ingredients

- oil spray
- 2 broccoli crowns, cut into florets
- 1 pinch salt
- parmesan cheese, as much or as little as you'd like

Instructions

- Give your air fryer a spritz of oil before placing in your broccoli florets.
- Give your broccoli a light spritz as well before sprinkling on some salt and grating some parmesan cheese on top.
- Set your air fryer on 400F for 5 minutes. Give the basket a little shake and then set the air fryer for another 5 minutes.
- Serve with your favourite meal!

Nutrition Info

3/4 cup: 272 calories, 16g fat (2g saturated fat), 0 cholesterol, 244mg sodium, 29g carbohydrate (5g sugars, 3g fiber), 5g protein.

Air Fryer Chicken Wings

Prep/Cook Time 30 minutes, Servings 24 wings

Ingredients

- 2 pounds chicken wings split and tips removed
- 1 ½ tablespoons flour

- 2 teaspoons baking powder
- ½ teaspoon seasoned salt
- ½ teaspoon black pepper

Instructions

- Preheat air fryer to 400°F.
- Pat wings dry with a paper towel. Combine flour, baking powder, salt and pepper and toss with wings. Shake off any excess flour mixture.
- Place wings in the air fryer in a single layer.
- Bake wings 20-22 minutes or until skin is crisp.
- Remove wings from air fryer and top with additional salt and pepper or desired sauce.

Nutrition Info

Calories: 47, Protein: 3g, Fat: 3g, Cholesterol: 15mg, Sodium: 63mg, Potassium: 65mg

Baked Eggs in Ramekins with Spinach and Cream

Prep/Cook Time: 30 minutes, Servings: 4 servings

Ingredients

- butter or nonstick spray
- 1 tablespoon olive oil
- 1 5-ounce bag baby spinach
- 1 garlic clove, minced
- 1/4 teaspoon kosher salt
- 4 large eggs
- 1/2 cup half and half
- freshly ground black pepper
- Maldon salt or other coarse, flaky sea salt
- toasted slices sourdough bread

Instructions

- Preheat the oven to 400 degrees F.
- Grease 4 6-ounce ramekins with butter or nonstick spray, and place on a rimmed baking sheet.
- Heat the olive oil in a large skillet over medium heat.

- Add the spinach and cook for about 5 minutes, stirring frequently, until the spinach is wilted and tender.
- Add the garlic and salt and cook, stirring, for 1-2 minutes more, until the garlic is fragrant.
- Divide the spinach between the ramekins.
- Crack an egg into a small bowl, then drop on top of the spinach. Repeat for the remaining ramekins. (Why do we not crack the eggs directly into the ramekins? Well, because if for some reason you've got a bad egg in the bunch, you've ruined that particular serving. Better to dirty one more bowl than to risk it.)
- Pour about 3 tablespoons half and half into each ramekin. You may not need all of it, since you shouldn't fill the ramekins the whole way to the top. Leave a little headroom, since the liquid will bubble as it cooks.
- Bake for about 12-15 minutes, until the yolks and the white immediately surrounding each yolk are just barely set and still have some jiggle to them. The eggs will continue to cook for a few minutes after they leave the oven.
- Grind black pepper and sprinkle coarse sea salt over each ramekin.
- Serve immediately with toasted slices of sourdough bread for dipping and spooning.

Nutrition Info

170 calories, 12g fat, 8mg cholesterol, 177mg sodium, 13g carbohydrate, 5g protein.

Air Fryer Turkey Bacon Recipe

Prep/Cook Time 35 mins, Servings: 8

Ingredients

- 1 package (about 8 ounces) Uncured Turkey Bacon

Instructions

- Preheat air fryer to 360F.
- Slice turkey bacon slices in half and place as many pieces that will fit in a single layer in air fryer basket.
- Cook for 5 minutes. Open air fryer and turn the bacon over.
- Place basket back in air fryer and continue to cook for 5 more minutes, or until bacon is cooked to your satisfaction.
- Repeat with remaining bacon pieces until it is all cooked.

Nutrition Info

Calories 30 Calories from Fat 14, Fat 1.5g, Protein 6g

Air Fryer Hash Browns

Prep/Cook Time 17 mins, Servings: 4

Ingredients

- 1/2 bag hash brown potatoes (470 calories per cup) I used Ore Ida
- spray oil
- salt and pepper

Instructions

- Place a vented parchment round in the basket of your air fryer.
- Add a thin layer of frozen hash browns.
- Sprinkle with salt and pepper (or other desired seasoning) then spray the top layer with oil.
- Cook for 7 minutes at 370°F, 165°C.
- Flip the hash browns and spritz with oil again.
- Cook for another 7-8 minutes or until desired color and texture are achieved.
- Plate and enjoy!

Nutrition Info

354 calories, 15g fat, 1mg cholesterol, 807mg sodium, 40g carbohydrate (7g sugars, 11g fiber), 17g protein.

Air Fryer Potato Wedges

Prep/Cook Time 20 minutes, Servings 2

Ingredients

- 2 russet potatoes (rinsed and dried)
- 1 teaspoon olive oil
- 1 teaspoon Kosher salt
- 1 teaspoon crushed rosemary
- 1 teaspoon crushed thyme leaves (if using ground, only use 1/4 to 1/2 teaspoon)
- cooking spray (optional)

Instructions

- Cut potatoes in half, then cut into wedges. Each potato should make 6-8 wedges depending on the thickness of the potatoes and the desired size of the wedge.
- In a large bowl, toss together potatoes with seasonings and olive oil.
- Spray the basket of the air fryer with cooking spray. Add the potatoes and if desired, spray potatoes with cooking spray for an extra crispy potato wedge.
- Set temperature to 390 degrees Fahrenheit and the timer for 15 minutes for regular sized wedges, adjust timing by a minute or two if the wedges are thinner or thicker.
- Want extra crispy wedges? Turn up the heat to 400 degrees Fahrenheit for an additional 2-3 minutes at the end of cooking time.
- Serve immediately.

Nutrition Info

Calories: 186kcal, Carbohydrates: 38g, Protein: 5g, Fat: 2g, Saturated Fat: 1g, Sodium: 1173mg, Potassium: 888mg, Fiber: 3g, Sugar: 1g

Air Fryer Tostones Recipe

Prep/Cook Time 20 minutes, 4 servings

Ingredients

Air-Fried Tostones

- 2 green plantains (~322g)
- 1 1/2 tablespoons avocado oil (or coconut oil or grapeseed oil)
- pinch of sea salt

Seasoning

- 1 cup warm water
- 3 garlic cloves, minced (or 2 teaspoons garlic powder)
- 1 teaspoon onion powder
- 2 teaspoons sea salt & pepper
- spray avocado oil

Instructions

- Set air-fryer to 420F.

- Peel the plantain by chopping off the ends and making a long slit along the side of the plantain, not too deep. Then peel off the skin.
- Chop the plantain into pieces no larger than 1-inch thick, then add them to the air-fryer basket, leaving adequate space between them.
- Air-fry for about 6 minutes or until golden brown. Remove from the air fryer.
- Mix together the seasoned water.
- Grab a coffee mug or bowl or flat surface and gently smash each piece of plantain to create the tostones.
- Dip the tostones in the seasoned water (one by one), then place it back in the air fryer basket. LET THEM DRY then spray them again with oil and place them back into the air fryer.
- Air fry for another 5 to 7 minutes, until the edges are golden brown and crispy. Pro-tip: I like to air fry mine for 4-5 minutes, then flip them over, and air-fry for an additional 2 – 3 minutes.
- Enjoy hot and fresh from the air fryer!

Nutrition Info

Calories 146, Protein 1g, Fat 6g, Carbs 24g

2 Ingredient Air Fryer Bagels

Prep/Cook Time: 20 mins, Servings: 4

Ingredients

- 1 cup self-rising flour
- 1 cup zero fat Greek yogurt, plain
- 1 egg (for egg wash) - optional
- Any desired bagel toppings such as poppy seeds, sesame seeds, etc.

Instructions

- Mix flour and yogurt in a mixing bowl. Combine into a tacky dough.
- Sprinkle flour onto a cutting board and roll dough into a ball. Cut dough ball into fourths.
- Using your hand, roll each dough ball into a bagel shape and pinch edges together.
- Place two at a time into a greased air fryer basket. Brush the tops of bagels with an egg wash (optional).
- Set the timer and cook for 10 minutes at 330 degrees Fahrenheit.

- Remove from air fryer. Brush with melted butter (optional) and season as desired.

Nutrition Info

134 calories, 6g fat (1g saturated fat), 0 cholesterol, 323mg sodium, 15g carbohydrate (4g sugars, 4g fiber), 4g protein.

Easy Air Fryer Donuts

Prep/Cook time 15 - 22 mins, Servings: 8 doughnuts

Ingredients

- 1/2 cup granulated sugar
- 1 tablespoon ground cinnamon
- 1 (16.3-ounce) can flaky large biscuits, such as Pillsbury Grands! Flaky Biscuits
- Olive oil spray or coconut oil spray
- 4 tablespoons unsalted butter, melted

Instructions

- Line a baking sheet with parchment paper. Combine sugar and cinnamon in a shallow bowl; set aside.
- Remove the biscuits from the can, separate them, and place them on the baking sheet. Use a 1-inch round biscuit cutter (or similarly-sized bottle cap) to cut holes out of the center of each biscuit.
- Lightly coat an air fryer basket with olive or coconut oil spray (do not use nonstick cooking spray such as Pam, which can damage the coating on the basket).
- Place 3 to 4 donuts in a single layer in the air fryer (they should not be touching). Close the air fryer and set to 350°F. Cook, flipping halfway through, until the donuts golden-brown, 5 to 6 minutes total. Transfer donuts place to the baking sheet. Repeat with the remaining biscuits. You can also cook the donut holes — they will take about 3 minutes total.
- Brush both sides of the warm donuts with melted butter, place in the cinnamon sugar, and flip to coat both sides. Serve warm.

Nutrition Info

77 calories, 5g fat, 299mg sodium, 7g carbohydrate (4g sugars, 3g fiber), 1g protein.

Air Fryer Potato Chips

Ingredients

- 1 medium Russet potato, unpeeled, cut into 1/8 inch thick slices (about 3/4 pound)
- 1 tablespoon canola oil
- 1/4 teaspoon sea salt
- 1/4 teaspoon freshly ground black pepper Canola oil
- 1 teaspoon chopped fresh rosemary

Instructions

- In a large bowl of cold water, soak potato slices for 20 minutes. Drain potatoes; pat dry with paper towels.
- Wipe bowl dry; then add oil, salt, and pepper. Add potatoes; toss gently to coat.
- Lightly coat air fryer basket with cooking spray. Place half of the potato slices in the basket, and cook in two batches at 375°F until cooked through and crispy, about 25 to 30 minutes.
- Using a pair of tongs, carefully remove chips from air fryer to plate. Sprinkle over rosemary; serve immediately or store in an airtight plastic container.

Nutrition Info

Calories 100, Fat 3.5g, Satfat 0g, Unsatfat 3.2g, Protein 2g, Carbohydrate 15g, Fiber 1g, Sugars 1g

Roast potatoes in a basket air fryer

Prep/Cook Time 45 minutes, Servings 4 servings

Ingredients

- 1.25 kg potato (3 lbs)
- 1 teaspoon oil

Instructions

- Wash potato, peel, cut into large chunks, adding chunks to a large bowl.

- Add 1 teaspoon of oil to the bowl of potato chunks and just using your clean hands, toss well until all surfaces are coated. (Tip! first have air basket pulled out and beside you, ready to receive the potatoes, because your hands will be oily.)
- Cook (no need to pre-heat) at 160 C (320 F) for 25 minutes.
- Take out the potatoes and tip them back into the bowl you have been using. Toss them in there briefly and gently using a large spoon.
- Transfer potato chunks back into fryer basket. Place back into machine, raise temperature on the machine to 180 C (350 F), and cook for another 7 minutes.
- Take out the potatoes and tip them back into the bowl you have been using. Toss them in there using a large spoon. (At this point, a few might look just about done, but once you toss them you'll see that there's loads that aren't quite as far along.)
- Transfer potato chunks back into fryer basket. Leave temperature unchanged. Roast for a final 7 minutes.
- Serve piping hot. Best reheated in machine.

Notes

Leftovers are best reheated in the air fryer as well, to restore their crispness to them. Try about 3 to 4 minutes at 160 C (320 F).

Nutrition Info

Calories: 250kcal, Protein: 6.3g, Fat: 1.5g, Sodium: 19mg, Fiber: 6.9g

Air Fryer Cracklin' Chicken

Prep/Cook Time 30 mins, Servings: 2 people

Ingredients

- 3 chicken thighs skin-on, and bone-in (1.25 pounds or less)
- Diamond Crystal kosher salt or your favorite cooking salt
- Magic Mushroom Powder (optional)

Instructions

- Grab some chicken thighs and a sharp pair of kitchen shears. Blot the chicken dry with a paper towel. If the thigh bone isn't exposed, use the shears to snip down to expose it. Then, starting at one end, carefully cut out the bone, making sure you don't cut through the meat.

- Trim as close to the bone as possible. When you get to the other end, trim around the joint and cartilage and remove the bone. Save these bones for homemade bone broth! Repeat with the remaining thighs.
- Flatten the chicken with a meat pounder to ensure uniform cooking.
- Sprinkle Diamond Crystal kosher salt on both sides of the chicken thighs. If you want to spice things up, you can sprinkle your favorite seasoning salt (e.g. Magic Mushroom Powder) on the meat side—but avoid sprinkling anything but salt on the skin side. (I don't recommend putting anything besides salt on the skin because the spices can burn.)
- Arrange the chicken thighs in a single layer in the the air fryer basket. You can actually smoosh up to three chicken thighs in a single layer in the air fryer basket without leaving any space in between them. They'll turn out fine—the pieces will shrink as they cook.
- Set the air fryer to 400°F for 15 to 18 minutes, depending on the size of the thighs. (My air fryer does not need to be preheated, but preheat yours if necessary.)
- The Cracklin' Chicken is ready when the skin is crispy and the meat is thoroughly cooked (at least 165°F in the thickest part of the thigh). If you're making another batch, pour out the rendered fat before cooking another batch to reduce the amount of smoke.

Nutrition Info

Calories: 371kcal, Carbohydrates: 1g, Protein: 28g, Fat: 28g

Garlic Roasted Potatoes with Paprika

Prep/Cook Time: 50 minutes, Servings: 4 servings

Ingredients

- 4 cups diced potatoes (1/2 inch cubes or smaller if you love them crispy!)
- 2 teaspoons olive oil
- 1 teaspoon kosher salt
- 1 teaspoon paprika
- 1/2 teaspoon garlic powder
- 1/2 teaspoon coarsely ground black pepper (reduce to 1/4 teaspoon if you have finely ground black pepper)
- 1/4 teaspoon onion powder

Instructions

- Preheat oven to 425°F.
- Toss diced potatoes with oil, salt, paprika, garlic powder, pepper, and onion powder until all potatoes are evenly coated with spices.
- Spread in an even, single layer on a rimmed baking sheet. Roast for 20 minutes, stir, and continue to roast for 15 minutes or until crispy on the outside and tender on the inside (baking time may vary slightly depending on how large or small you cut your potatoes).
- Enjoy immediately.

Notes

- To prepare in air fryer, reduce olive oil to 1/2 teaspoon. Cook in air fryer at 350°F for 15 minutes or until crispy on outside and soft on the inside, tossing/shaking basket once or twice during cooking time.
- You can reduce the salt in this recipe if you're watching sodium in your diet. They taste best with this amount of salt, but as always, adjust for your personal needs.
- This recipe also works great with sweet potatoes!
- If desired, add diced onions halfway through cooking time.
- If you have a convection setting on your oven, use it for extra crispiness!
- Reheating Instructions: To restore the crispiness of these, reheat in oven or toaster oven preheated to 425°F for 5 minutes or until crispy and warmed through. You can also reheat these in a dry frying pan over medium high heat, stirring or tossing frequently, for 5 minutes or until crispy and warmed through. Microwave is not recommended! Unless you like soggy potatoes.

Nutrition Info

Calories: 139, Total Fat: 3g, Saturated Fat: 0g, Cholesterol: 0mg, Sodium: 291mg, Carbohydrates: 27g, Fiber: 4g, Sugar: 1g, Protein: 3g

Air Fryer (or Oven) Roasted Carrots with Moroccan Spice Mix

Prep/Cook Time 24 minutes, Servings 4 servings

Ingredients

Carrots Ingredients:

- 1 lb. carrots, peeled and sliced in diagonal pieces. Organic whole carrots are best for this.
- 2 T olive oil (or slightly less for air fryer, but you need the oil to make the spice mix stick to the carrots)
- 1/2 tsp. salt
- fresh ground black pepper to taste

Moroccan Spice Mix Ingredients:

- This makes enough for 5 batches of roasted veggies. Store leftover spice mix in a small glass jar.
- 2 tsp. ground cumin
- 1 tsp. ground coriander
- 1/2 tsp. chile powder, see notes
- 1/2 tsp. sweet paprika
- 1/2 tsp. ground cinnamon
- 1/4 tsp. ground allspice
- 1/4 tsp. ground ginger
- 1/8 tsp. cayenne pepper
- pinch of ground cloves, optional

Instructions

Air Fryer Instructions:

- Peel carrots and cut into diagonal slices, cutting thicker parts of the carrot in half before you slice them diagonally so you have carrots that are about the same length and thickness.
- Mix ground cumin, ground coriander, chile powder, sweet paprika, ground cinnamon, ground allspice, ground ginger, cayenne pepper, and cloves to make the spice mix.
- Start preheating the Air Fryer to 360F/185C if your Air Fryer needs to be preheated.
- Toss carrots with olive oil, salt, fresh-ground black pepper, and 1 tsp. of the spice mix.

- Spread carrots out in a single layer in the Air Fryer basket.
- Cook carrots 7-8 minutes; then remove basket and check them, flipping carrots over to the other side.
- Put the basket back into Air Fryer and cook carrots about 5-6 minutes more. (I would check after a few minutes; some air fryers cook more quickly than others.)

Oven Instructions:

- Preheat oven to 475F/250C. (Or use 450F/230C if you're cooking in a toaster oven which doesn't go that high. Use a convection oven if you have one.)
- Peel and cut carrots, make spice mix, and toss carrots with olive oil and spices as above.
- Cover shallow roasting pan with foil or spray with non-stick spray or olive oil.
- Arrange carrots in a single layer on pan.
- Roast 20-25 minutes, turning every 10 minutes, or until carrots are starting to brown and are slightly shriveled. Serve immediately.

Nutrition Info

Calories: 99, Total Fat: 7g, Saturated Fat: 1g, Unsaturated Fat: 5.7g, Cholesterol: 0mg, Sodium: 357mg, Carbohydrates: 9.3g, Fiber: 3.4g, Sugar: 3.9g, Protein: 9g

Air Fryer Brussel Sprouts

Prep/Cook Time 15 mins, Servings: 4 people

Ingredients

- 3 c halved brussel sprouts
- 1 T olive oil
- 1/4 t salt
- 1/4 t pepper

Instructions

- Toss brussel sprouts with olive and salt/pepper.
- Place into air fryer basket.
- Set air fryer for 400 degrees F and cook 8-12 minutes.
- ENJOY!

Nutrition Info

Calories: 31kcal, Fat: 3g, Sodium: 145mg

Delicious and Easy Oven Roasted Broccoli

Prep/Cook Time: 20 mins, Servings: 6

Ingredients

- 1 head of broccoli (double if cooking for more than 2 or 3)
- 2 tablespoons of extra virgin olive oil
- salt and pepper to taste

Instructions

- Preheat your oven or toaster oven to 425° F.
- Start by washing a head of broccoli and cutting into uniform pieces...they don't all have to be the same size, but mostly similar.
- Place the broccoli on a sheet pan in a single layer.Next, drizzle with extra virgin olive oil. Then, season well with salt and pepper or some sort of seasoning. I love using steak seasoning on broccoli because it contains coarse salt, pepper and garlic.
- Place in your oven or toaster oven and set a time for 6 minutes. Once 6 minutes is up, use some tongs to toss the broccoli around a bit. Cook for 6 more minutes, then test for doneness. It' going to be up to you how done you like your broccoli. I typically cook mine for 18 minutes to get it just how I like it!
- Remove from the oven and serve immediately!

Nutrition Info

165 calories, 5g fat (1g saturated fat), 23mg cholesterol, 707mg sodium, 16g carbohydrate (4g sugars, 4g fiber), 8g protein

5 Ingredient Crispy Air fryer Chicken Tenders

Prep/Cook Time: 25 minutes, Servings: 4

Ingredients

- 2 large boneless skinless chicken breasts, sliced into tenders
- 1 cup panko breadcrumbs (plus more if needed)
- 1 egg
- 1/4 cup flour
- non-stick cooking spray

Instructions

- In 3 separate bowls, add the flour, panko and egg.
- In the bowl with the egg, add 1 tablespoon of water and whisk with a fork to make an egg wash.
- Season the flour with salt and pepper.
- Bread the chicken tenders one at a time by first dredging them in the flour, then the egg wash and then coat them with breadrumbs.
- Place the breaded tenders in the airfry basket and spray both sides of the chicken with a light coating of cooking spray.
- Pre-heat your oven on the air fryer mode set to 415 degrees.
- Place the chicken tenders in the oven set for 15 minutes.
- Turn the tenders over halfway through the cooking time.
- Remove when cooked through (check with a thermometer) and immediately sprinkle with kosher salt.
- Serve with your favorite dipping sauce like ranch, bbq, or even just a squeeze of fresh lemon.

Nutrition Info

210 calories, 21g carbohydrate, 9g protein

Lemon Tempeh Air Fryer Sheet Pan

Prep/Cook Time 40 mins, Marinating 2 hours, Servings 2

Ingredients

- 1/4 cup lemon juice
- 2 tablespoons low sodium soy sauce (may use gluten-free tamari)
- 2 cloves garlic minced or pressed
- 1/2 teaspoon tahini (optional)
- 1/2 teaspoon dried thyme leaves
- 1/4 teaspoon freshly ground black pepper
- 8 drops monk fruit or other liquid sweetener (may use a teaspoon of sugar)

Tempeh and Vegetables

- 8 ounces tempeh cut into 32 cubes
- 14 ounces asparagus (one bunch)
- 8 ounces mushrooms (baby bella or white button mushrooms)
- 1 large red bell pepper
- 1 1/2 cups cooked rice
- Tahini-Chickpea Dressing or dressing of choice

Suggested Tools

Breville Smart Oven Air

Instructions

- In a large bowl, whisk the marinade ingredients together until well-blended. Add the cubed tempeh and gently stir to coat. Cover and allow to marinate in the refrigerator for at least 2 hours, up to overnight, stirring occasionally.
- Prepare the vegetables: Snap off the tough ends of asparagus, slice the bell pepper, and halve the mushrooms (quarter them if they're large.)
- Drain the marinade from the tempeh into a rectangular baking dish. (Do not throw it out.) Add the asparagus to the marinade and toss to coat. Lift the asparagus out of the marinade and place it on a plate. Repeat with the mushrooms and bell pepper. If you're running low on marinade, freshen it up with a splash of lemon juice.

For Breville Smart Oven Air

- Follow the Preparation Instructions above. Set the Breville to the Air Fryer setting, place the basket on the appropriate level, and set the temperature to 450F and time to 16 minutes.
- Once the oven is pre-heated, add the tempeh in a single layer to one side of the basket. Air fry for 7 minutes, but don't turn off the oven. Add the asparagus and peppers to another section of the pan, and air fry for 4 more minutes. Add the mushrooms and air-fry for 4-6 minutes or until they are tender. If anything starts to get over-cooked, remove it from the air fryer. If anything is under-cooked, give it more time. (Larger asparagus spears may take more time, while very thin spears will take less.)
- Remove the tempeh and vegetables from the air fryer and serve over rice, drizzled with tahini sauce or your choice of dressing.

In the Oven

- Follow the Preparation Instructions above. Preheat oven to 350F. Line a baking sheet with parchment paper. Place the tempeh on one side of the pan in a single layer. When the oven is hot, put the pan in and set a timer for 8 minutes.

- After 8 minutes, turn the tempeh with a spatula and add the vegetables to the other side of the baking sheet, in a single layer. Bake for 8-10 more minutes, until the tempeh is beginning to crisp along the edges and the vegetables are tender but not over-cooked. If any one food needs more time, remove the others so they don't get over-cooked.
- Serve over rice with your choice of dressing.

Nutrition Info

Calories 463 Calories from Fat 63, Fat 7g, Saturated Fat 1.7g, Carbohydrates 70g, Fiber 17g, Sugar 11g, Protein 35g

The Best Easy Air Fryer French Fries Recipe

Prep/Cook Time: 1 hour 5 minutes, Servings: 6

Ingredients

- 3 large russet potatoes
- 2-3 tablespoons olive oil
- Sea salt and pepper, to taste

Instructions

- Using a mandoline, slice the potatoes into fries. I don't worry too much about the size of fry I am making- some are bigger, and some are smaller. That's fine!
- Next, place your spuds in a nice cool water bath. Completely submerge the fries in water.
- Let fries sit one hour. This helps to remove excess starch and will help the fries crisp up more in the oven.
- Preheat air fryer to 375 degrees.
- After an hour, drain the water, and pat fries dry with a paper towel.
- Toss with a couple tablespoons of olive oil, salt and pepper.
- Add fries to bottom of air fryer basket, making sure they are all on the same level (don't stack them on top of each other.)
- Cook 13 minutes, until crispy and golden brown.
- Place on a baking sheet lined with paper towels and a cooling rack over it.
- Place in warm oven (set to the minimum temperature, not over 250 degrees) and let rest while other batches of fries are cooking.
- Serve hot and enjoy.

Nutrition Info

Calories 205, Total Fat 7g, Saturated Fat 1g, Unsaturated Fat 6g, Cholesterol 0mg, Sodium 70mg, Carbohydrates 32g

Air Fryer Whole Chicken

Ingredients

- 1 whole chicken
- 1 tbsp dry rub
- salt optional
- calorie controlled cooking spray or olive oil

Instructions

Make your Air Fryer Whole Chicken

- Preheat the air fryer to 180C / 350F.
- Pat chicken dry. Rub in the dry rub and sprinkle salt if desired.
- Spray air fryer with cooking spray.
- Add chicken in and cook for 30 mins on one side.
- Then flip and cook for 15-30 mins on other side depending on the size of your bird.
- It is important to check that the internal temperature of the chicken is 75C (165F) before serving.

Nutrition Info

Calories: 412kcal, Protein: 35g, Fat: 28g, Saturated Fat: 8g, Cholesterol: 142mg, Sodium: 133mg, Potassium: 359mg

Air Fryer Avocado Fries

Prep/Cook Time 12 minutes, 4 Serving

Ingredients

- 3 avocados, peeled and sliced
- 1 cup panko breadcrumbs
- 1/4 cup flour of choice
- 1 egg, lightly beaten
- 1/4 tsp dark chili powder
- 1/4 tsp hot paprika
- 1/4 tsp garlic powder

- 1/4 tsp kosher salt
- Avocado oil spray
- Serve with: dip of choice

Instructions

- In a small dish add the flour, chili powder, paprika, garlic powder, and kosher salt. Stir to combine. In another small dish add the egg and beat until frothy. In another dish add the panko breadcrumbs.
- In an assembly line manner, roll the first avocado slice in the flour (give it a light tap to remove excess flour), then submerge it in the egg wash, followed by the panko bread crumbs. I gently push the panko into the avocado to ensure its evenly coated. Repeat with all of the avocado slices.
- Lightly grease the air fryer basket with avocado spray, then place the avocado fries with some space in between, then lightly spray the fries with some avocado oil. Air fry on 390F for 7 minutes, flipping halfway through, or until desired crispiness. Depending on the size of your air fryer basket, will depend on how many batches you have to do.

Notes

- Slicing avocado: Cut avocado in half and carefully remove the seed. Then gently insert your thumb in between the skin and flesh to peel the skin off. Place avocado flat side down and cut the avocado into slices.
- Favorite types of dipping sauce for this recipe: buffalo ranch, plain ranch, chipotle aioli, or hot sauce.
- Oven instructions: Preheat the oven to 425F. Grease baking sheet, place panko breaded avocado fries on baking sheet, spray the top with a little avocado spray. Bake the avocado fries for 15 minutes, flipping halfway through, or until they are golden and crispy.

Nutrition Info

Calories: 447, Total Fat: 31g, Saturated Fat: 5g, Trans Fat: 0g, Unsaturated Fat: 24g, Cholesterol: 50mg, Sodium: 314mg, Carbohydrates: 39g, Fiber: 12g, Sugar: 3g, Protein: 9g

Southwestern Roasted Corn

Ingredients

- 1 1/2 cups (246 g) Frozen Corn Kernels, (do not defrost)
- 1 cup (160 g) onions, chopped
- 1 cup (149 g) diced mixed bell peppers
- 1 (1) diced jalapeno pepper
- 1 tsp (1 tsp) Ground Cumin
- 1 tbsp (1 tbsp) Lemon Juice
- 1/2 tsp (0.5 tsp) Kosher Salt
- 1/2 tsp (0.5 tsp) Ancho Chile Powder
- 1/4 cup (30.5 g) queso fresco, or feta cheese
- 1/4 cup (4 g) Chopped Cilantro or Parsley
- 1 tbsp (1 tbsp) Lemon Juice

Instructions

- In a large bowl, combine corn, onions, bell peppers, and jalapenos, and stir.
- Sprinkle in 1 tablespoon lemon juice and add all the spices. The lemon juice will help the dry spices stick to the vegetables.
- Pour the spiced vegetables into the air fryer basket.
- Set your airfryer to 400F for 10 minutes and stir halfway.
- Add queso fresco (or cotija, or feta cheese), chopped cilantro and the remaining 1 tablespoon of lemon juice and mix well before serving.

Nutrition Info

Calories: 104kcal, Carbohydrates: 18g, Protein: 3g, Fat: 2g, Fiber: 2g, Sugar: 5g

Prep/Cook Time: 55 minutes, Servings: 2

Ingredients

- 2 sweet potatoes, (medium size, about 8 oz each)
- 1/2 teaspoon oil, (like coconut oil, olive oil, avocado oil or canola oil)

Instructions

- Adjust the toaster oven cooking rack to the lowest position and preheat to 400°F on the "Bake" setting.
- Insert an oven-safe rack inside of a rimmed toaster oven baking sheet.
- Wash the sweet potatoes, scrubbing the skin well and dry completely with a kitchen towel. Stab each sweet potato with a sharp knife or fork a few times, rub with oil and place on the rack in the prepared baking sheet.
- Bake until a knife slides easily into the sides of the sweet potatoes, about 45 to 55 minutes for medium potatoes.
- The sweet potatoes will be hot, allow them to rest 5 to 10 minutes before handling. To serve slice a line across the top of the sweet potatoes, push the edges towards the center to puff them up and fluff the interior with a fork.

Nutrition Info

Calories: 215, Total Fat: 1.5g, Saturated Fat: 1g, Sodium: 82mg, Carbohydrates: 47g, Fiber: 7.6g, Sugar: 14.7g, Protein: 4.6g

Tender & Juicy Whole Chicken

Prep/Cook Time: 58 minutes, Servings: 4

Ingredients

- 1 Whole chicken washed, neck removed
- 2 Apples sliced
- 1/2 c baby carrots
- 1/2 c sliced onions
- 1 Bay Leaf
- 1 Garlic Clove
- 1/4 c olive oil
- 1/2 tsp Garlic Salt
- 1/2 tsp Sea Salt
- 1/2 tsp Rosemary
- 1/2 tsp Sugar
- 1/2 tsp Turmeric
- 1/2 tsp Paprika

Instructions

- Remove and discard insides of chicken. Rinse chicken with cold water and pat dry. Trim away any excess fat.
- Combine spices in a small bowl and sprinkle over chicken and into the cavity.
- Place Carrots, Apples, garlic clove and bay leaf in the body cavity!
- Place chicken, breast side up, on a broiler pan (or on a rack inside another pan) coated with cooking spray.
- Bake at 400 degrees for 45 minutes or until meat thermometer inserted into thigh registers 165 degrees.
- Remove the veggies inside the cavity and place in a bowl, allowing the Chicken rest for 10 minutes before serving!

Nutrition Info

195 calories, 6g fat (2g saturated fat), 9mg cholesterol, 382mg sodium, 33g carbohydrate (6g sugars, 2g fiber), 4g protein.

Convection Oven Roast Chicken

Prep/Cook Time: 1hr 20mins, SERVES: 4

Ingredients

- 1 (5 lb) roasting chickens
- 3/4 teaspoon kosher salt
- 1/2 teaspoon fresh ground black pepper
- fresh herb (rosemary, thyme, oregano, marjoram, etc.,1/4-inch sprig)
- 1 garlic clove, peeled and cut in half
- 1 small onion, peeled and quartered (about 2 ounces)
- 4 slices lemon zest (1/2-x-3-inches each)
- 1 tablespoon extra virgin olive oil
- 1 tablespoon fresh lemon juice

Instructions

- Place the toaster oven rack to the lowest position in the oven. Preheat the oven to 400°F on the convection setting.
- Remove giblets and neck from cavity of chicken, reserve for another use or discard. Rinse chicken with cold water and pat dry.
- Place a baking rack into the broiling pan (that is lined with foil) add 1/4 cup water to the pan and lightly spray the baking rack with cooking spray.
- Tuck the wings under and place the chicken on the baking rack pan. Clean work surface and hands with soap and hot water before continuing.
- Combine the salt and pepper. Rub half the mixture in the cavity of the chicken; then place the herb sprig(s), garlic halves, onion quarters and lemon zest in the cavity of the chicken.
- Loosely tie the legs together. Rub the chicken with the olive oil and remaining salt and pepper. Drizzle with the lemon juice.
- Place the chicken in the oven and roast at 400°F for 20 minutes, then lower the temperature to 375°F and continue to roast for an additional 12 minutes per pound longer.
- Considering my chicken was 5 lbs. I will roast it for 60 minutes. You will have to calculate the time according to your chicken's weight by multiplying 12 minutes times the size per pound of your chicken.
- The Internal temperature of the chicken should be 170°F when tested in the breast, and 180°F when tested in the dark meat.
- Juices should run clear.

- Turn off oven and remove the chicken to a platter. Let stand 10 - 15 minutes before carving (may cover loosely with foil if desired, but skin will lose its crispness).

Nutrition Info

225 calories, 2g fat (1g saturated fat), 21mg cholesterol, 695mg sodium, 30g carbohydrate (5g sugars, 9g fiber), 18g protein.

Air Fryer Rotisserie Chicken

Prep/Cook Time: 1 hour 5 minutes, Servings: 4 servings

Ingredients

- 1 Whole Chicken cleaned and blotted dry
- 2 Tablespoons Ghee (or high quality Coconut Oil or Olive Oil)
- 1 Tablespoon TOG House Seasoning

Instructions

- Remove giblet packet from chicken and pat dry.
- Rub Ghee/Oil all over chicken and season generously.
- Place chicken, breast side down into Air Fryer basket.
- Cook at 350 degrees for 30 minutes.
- Flip chicken over and cook for 350 degrees for an additional 30 minutes, or until internal temperature reaches 165 degrees.
- Let rest for 10 minutes and then serve.

Nutrition Info

Calories 475 Calories from Fat 324, Saturated Fat 12g, Potassium 359mg, Carbohydrates 0g, Sugar 0g, Protein 35g

Air Fryer Honey Garlic Chicken Wings

Prep/Cook Time: 45 minutes, Servings: 2 servings

Ingredients

- 16 Pieces Chicken Wings
- 3/4 cup Potato Starch
- 1/4 cup Clover Honey
- 1/4 cup Butter
- 4 Tablespoons Fresh Garlic minced
- 1/2 teaspoon Kosher Salt
- 1/8 cup Fresh Water (or more as needed)

Instructions

- Rinse and dry chicken wings. Add Potato Starch to bowl and coat chicken wings. Add coated chicken wings to Air Fryer.
- Cook at 380 degrees for 25 minutes, shaking the basket every five minutes.
- When Timer sounds, cook at 400 degrees for 5-10 minutes. All skin on all wings should be very dry and crisp.
- Heat a small stainless steel saucepan on low heat. Melt butter and then add garlic. Sauté the garlic for 5 minutes.
- Add honey and salt and simmer on low for about 20 minutes, stirring every few minutes, just so the sauce does not burn. Add a few drops of water after 15 minutes to keep Sauce from hardening.
- Remove chicken wings from Air Fryer and pour over the sauce.

Nutrition Info

195 calories, 10g fat, 6mg cholesterol, 157mg sodium, 27g carbohydrate, 2g protein.

Air Fried Chicken Drumsticks

Prep/Cook Time: 30 minutes, Servings 8

Ingredients

- 8 chicken drumsticks
- 2 tbsp olive oil
- 1 tsp celtic sea salt

- 1 tsp fresh cracked pepper
- 1 tsp garlic powder
- 1 tsp paprika
- 1/2 tsp cumin

Instructions

- In a small bowl, combine herbs and spices.
- Set aside.
- Place drumsticks in a bowl or a plastic bag and drizzle with olive oil.
- Toss to coat.
- Sprinkle herbs and spices all over drumsticks to coat them.
- Preheat air fryer at 400 for 2-10 minutes.
- Place drumsticks in air fryer basket and cook for 10 minutes on 400.
- Remove basket and flip chicken drumsticks.
- Cook at 400 for another 10 minutes.
- If chicken is not 165 degrees internally, add another 5 minutes of cook-time.
- Time can vary based on drumstick size, so do check the temperature with a digital thermometer after cooking to prevent over or under cooking.
- When chicken has reached 165 degrees internally, serve immediately.

Nutrition Info

Calories 201, Total Fat 12g, Saturated Fat 3g, Trans Fat 0g, Unsaturated Fat 8g, Cholesterol 116mg, Sodium 381mg, Carbohydrates 1g, Fiber 0g, Sugar 0g, Protein 22g

Air Fryer, Chinese Salt and Pepper Chicken Wings

Prep/Cook Time: 45, Servings: 6 servings

Ingredients

- 1 pound chicken wings
- 1 egg white
- 1 teaspoon salt
- 1 teaspoon black pepper

Instructions

- Start by cracking the egg white in a large mixing bowl, beat until frothy, add in the salt and pepper.

- Add the chicken wing pieces into the bowl, and allow them to sit for about 15 minutes.
- Set them in a single layer in the air fryer basket.
- Set the temperature for 380 degrees for 12 minutes, after 12 minutes, using tongs flip the chicken wings.
- Then increase the temperature to 400 degrees F, for another 5 minutes.
- Plate, serve and enjoy!

Nutrition Info

308 calories, 10g fat, 47mg cholesterol, 704mg sodium, 31g carbohydrate, 24g protein.

Crispy Air Fried Chicken Breasts (Keto/Low Carb)

Prep/Cook Time: 30 M

ingredients:

- 1 egg
- 2 Tbsp heavy whipping cream
- 3.5 ounce pork rinds, crushed (about 1 1/2 to 2 cups when crushed)
- 1/4 cup Parmesan cheese
- 1 tsp kosher salt
- 1 tsp garlic powder
- 1 tsp Italian seasoning
- 1/4 tsp red pepper flakes
- 2 large chicken breasts, chilled & patted dry (approximately 2 lbs), split in half to make 4 thinner chicken breasts

Instructions:

- Preheat air fryer to 400°F
- If your chicken breasts are thick, slice in half through the middle like you would butterfly the chicken breasts only you go all the way through to make two thinner breasts. (Refer to picture #1 above)
- Create an assembly line of sorts to bread the chicken by laying out 2 containers and a baking tray with a rack.
- In one container add your egg mixture - 1 egg whisked with 2 tablespoons heavy whipping cream
- In the other container add your breading mixture - 3.5 ounce pork rinds, crushed (1 1/2 to 2 cups), 1/4 cup Parmesan cheese, 1 tsp kosher salt, 1 tsp

garlic powder, 1 tsp Italian seasoning, & 1/4 tsp red pepper flakes. Stir to mix well.

• Pat chicken dry. Dip one chicken breast in the egg mixture to coat both sides. Then dredge the coated chicken breast in the bread crumb mixture being sure to completely bread both sides. Place breaded chicken breast on rack in baking sheet until ready to air fry. Continue to bread all 4 pieces of chicken. TIP: Line the baking tray with foil for easy clean-up.

• Brush the air fryer basket with oil or use cooking spray per Instructions for your air fryer

• Place breaded chicken in air fryer basket in a single layer and air fry for 14-16 minutes or until no longer pink in the middle and an instant read thermometer reads 150°F. Air fry remaining chicken in same manner until all chicken is cooked through.

• Allow chicken to rest for 5-10 minutes before serving. Enjoy!

NOTES:

• A food processor makes quick work of crushing the pork rinds, but you can also crush them in a baggie using your hands, a rolling pin, or a heavy skillet

• For easy clean-up I lay paper towels under the containers at my breading station

• Line the baking tray with foil for easy clean up. This will catch any breading crumbs that fall through the rack while breading the chicken

• Be sure your chicken is chilled. Remove chicken from fridge right before you plan to bread it. This will help the breading stick

• Pat the chicken dry before breading.

• Be sure to place chicken in air fryer basket in single layer. DON'T STACK THE CHICKEN. If you stack chicken they will not get crispy.

• When air frying the chicken, keep the air fryer closed. No need to turn the chicken or shake the basket when making air fried chicken breasts

Nutrition Info

Calories 505.17, Fat (grams) 19.88, Sat. Fat (grams) 7.73, Carbs (grams) 1.91, Sugar (grams) 0.31, Protein (grams) 74.78, Sodium (milligrams) 1299.06, Cholesterol (grams) 236.94

Garlic Parmesan Chicken Wings in an Air Fryer

Ingredients

- 2 pounds chicken wings (or drumsticks)
- 3/4 cup grated Parmesan cheese
- 2 teaspoons minced garlic
- 2 teaspoons fresh parsley (chopped)
- 1 teaspoon salt
- 1 teaspoon pepper

Instructions

- Preheat your air fryer to 400 degrees for 3-4 minutes
- Pat chicken pieces dry with a paper towel.
- Mix Parmesan cheese, garlic, parsley, salt, and pepper together in a bowl.
- Toss chicken pieces in cheese mixture until coated.
- Place chicken in bottom of air fryer basket and set timer to 10-12 minutes.
- After 12 minutes, use tongs to flip chicken.
- Fry again for 12 minutes.
- Remove chicken from basket with tongs and sprinkle with more Parmesan cheese and parsley.
- Serve with your favorite dipping sauce. We like ranch, and buffalo.

Nutrition Info

244 calories, 9g fat (1g saturated fat), 0 cholesterol, 454mg sodium, 30g carbohydrate (3g sugars, 8g fiber), 9g protein.

Air Fryer Bacon Wrapped Jalapeño Chicken Poppers

Prep/Cook Time: 44 minutes, Servings: 8 pieces

Ingredients

- 8 Jalapeño Peppers cleaned and cut in half
- 3/4 cup Cream Cheese
- 3/4 cup Monterey Jack Cheese (or other melting cheese) shredded
- 1 Scallion chopped
- 2 Chicken Breasts Boneless/Skinless pounded and cut into 8 strips

- 1/4 teaspoon TOG House Seasoning
- 8 slices Bacon
- 1/2 cup Korean Style BBQ Sauce
- or
- 1/2 cup Barbecue Sauce

Instructions

- Slice off tops and stems of jalapeño peppers. Make a slit in each jalapeno pepper along one side and carefully remove the membrane and seeds.
- Mix together cream cheese, cheese, scallions and salt and stuff inside each jalapeño peppers.
- Pound chicken into 8 flat strips and season with TOG Seasoning.
- Wrap one chicken strip around each jalapeño popper.
- Wrap one slice of bacon around each chicken jalapeño, trying to seal the opening (with chicken or bacon) and secure with a toothpick.
- Add 2 Tablespoons of water into air fryer drawer. Place poppers in air fryer basket and then into drawer and cook at 340 degrees for 24 minutes (depending on size), turning over half way through.
- Brush Barbecue Sauce on each popper and cook at 390 degrees for 5 minutes, or until bubbly.

Nutrition Info

Calories 206 Calories from Fat 90, Fat 10g, Saturated Fat 3g, Cholesterol 35mg, Sodium 863mg, Potassium 291mg, Carbohydrates 15g, Fiber 1g, Sugar 12g, Protein 13g

Vegan Spicy Fried "Chicken" Soy Curls

Prep/Cook Time 32 minutes, Servings 2

Ingredients

- 60 grams soy curls (about 1 1/2 cups)
- 2 cups hot water
- 1 1/2 teaspoons no-chicken bouillon
- 1/4 teaspoon chipotle chili powder (or to taste)
- freshly ground black pepper generously, to taste

Coating Ingredients

- 2 tablespoons cornmeal

- 2 tablespoons whole wheat flour
- 1 tablespoon Nutrition Infoal yeast
- 1-2 teaspoons creole seasoning (use more or less to taste)
- 1/4 teaspoon poultry seasoning
- 1/4 teaspoon chipotle powder (use smoked paprika to reduce spiciness)
- 1 tablespoon plain non-dairy yogurt (or 2 1/2 teaspoons non-dairy milk and 1/2 teaspoon lemon juice)
- 1 tablespoon hot sauce

Instructions

- Put the soy curls in a saucepan over medium-high heat. Stir in the hot or boiling water, bouillon, 1/4 teaspoon chipotle pepper, and black pepper. Bring to a boil and cook for a few minutes, until the soy curls have softened. Remove from the heat and set aside while you mix the coating ingredients.
- Combine the dry coating ingredients in a small bowl. Whisk the yogurt and hot sauce together in a large bowl (large enough to hold the soy curls.)
- Place the air fryer basket in the air fryer. If you're using an oven, put a baking sheet into the oven. Preheat your air fryer/oven. For the Breville Air, use the air frying setting and set the temperature to 425F. For a regular air fryer or oven, set the temperature to 400F.
- Using a colander, drain the soy curls (you can keep the liquid and use it to add salt and flavor to soups and gravies if you want.) Use the back of a large spoon to press as much liquid as you can out of the soy curls.
- Pour the soy curls into the bowl with the yogurt mixture and toss well to coat. Sprinkle the dry mix onto the curls a little at a time as you stir to make sure they're all evenly coated.
- Place perforated parchment paper in your air fryer basket or regular parchment paper on your baking sheet. Pour the soy curls onto the paper and spread them out so that they aren't touching.
- In the Breville or air fryer, cook for 6 minutes and then shake the basket or stir to shift them around. (At this point in the Breville, I was able to remove the parchment paper without them sticking.) Cook for 5-7 more minutes, until the soy curls are crispy on the outside.
- In the oven, cook for 10 minutes and then turn the soy curls over as best you can, breaking up any that have stuck together. Cook for 10-15 more minutes, until the soy curls are crispy on the outside.
- Serve with your choice of dipping sauces or on a salad with ranch dressing.

Nutrition Info

Calories 172 Calories from Fat 45, Fat 5g, Sodium 745mg, Carbohydrates 19g, Fiber 5g, Sugar 1g, Protein 13g

Perfect Air Fryer Steak

Ingredients

- New York Strip Steak 1 1/4 inches thick, around 1 lb. (size depends on your preference)
- salt
- pepper
- Weber Steak Seasoning (optional instead of salt and pepper)

Instructions

- Start by bringing the steaks to room temperature. It's super important not too cook steaks when they are cold so they cook evenly on the inside and out. It usually takes 30 minutes to an hour for steaks to get to room temperature.
- Once your steaks have come to room temp, it's time to season them. I like to keep it simple and season them with salt and pepper or Weber Steak Seasoning
- Preheat your air fryer to 400° F. Once the air fryer is ready, place the steaks on the rack or basket at least an inch apart so the air can circulate around them. Cook for 12-24 minutes, flipping midway through. Use a meat thermometer to check the temperature.
- The safe temperature for cooked beef is 145° Fahrenheit, but most people prefer their cakes cooked differently. I typically love my steaks cooked medium-rare to medium.
- Once you pull your steaks from the air fryer, place them on a plate or pan with aluminum foil lightly tenting them, and allow them to rest for 10 minutes.
- Slice and serve.

Nutrition Info

76 calories, 5g fat, 105mg sodium, 8g carbohydrate, 3g protein.

Air-Fryer Ground Beef Wellington

Prep/Cook: 50 min., 2 servings

Ingredients

- 1/2 cup chopped fresh mushrooms
- 1 tablespoon butter
- 2 teaspoons all-purpose flour
- 1/4 teaspoon pepper, divided
- 1/2 cup half-and-half cream
- 1 large egg yolk
- 2 tablespoons finely chopped onion
- 1/4 teaspoon salt
- 1/2 pound ground beef
- 1 tube (4 ounces) refrigerated crescent rolls
- 1 large egg, lightly beaten, optional
- 1 teaspoon dried parsley flakes

Instructions

- Preheat air fryer to 300°. In a saucepan, heat butter over medium-high heat. Add mushrooms; cook and stir until tender, 5-6 minutes. Stir in flour and 1/8 teaspoon pepper until blended. Gradually add cream. Bring to a boil; cook and stir for 2 minutes or until thickened. Remove from the heat and set aside.
- In a bowl, combine egg yolk, onion, 2 tablespoons mushroom sauce, salt and remaining 1/8 teaspoon pepper. Crumble beef over mixture and mix well. Shape into 2 loaves. Unroll crescent dough and separate into 2 rectangles; press perforations to seal. Place meat loaf on each rectangle. Bring edges together and pinch to seal. If desired, brush with beaten egg.
- Place Wellingtons in a single layer on greased tray in air-fryer basket. Cook until golden brown and a thermometer inserted into meat loaf reads 160°, 18-22 minutes.
- Meanwhile, warm remaining sauce over low heat; stir in parsley. Serve sauce with Wellingtons.

Nutrition Info

1 serving: 585 calories, 38g fat, 208mg cholesterol, 865mg sodium, 30g carbohydrate, 29g protein.

Air Fryer Steak with Herb Lemon Butter

Prep/Cook Time: 17 mins, Servings: 2

Ingredients

Herb Lemon Butter

- 1/2 stick unsalted butter at room temperature
- 3 tbsp fresh parsley chopped
- 1 tsp thyme chopped
- 1/2 tsp lemon zest
- salt
- black pepper

Steak

- 2 (8oz) steak
- 2 tsp olive oil

Instructions

To Make Herb Lemon Butter:

- Mix together butter, parsley, thyme, lemon zest, salt and pepper in a small bowl.
- Transfer mixture to parchment paper and form into a log shape.
- Roll the butter in the parchment to 1 1/2 inches in diameter, twisting the ends to close and refrigerate until later.

To Make Steak In Air Fryer:

- Preheat air fryer to 400F / 200C.
- Rub the olive oil on both side of the steaks and season with salt and black pepper.
- Add the steaks to the air fryer and cook for 12 mins for medium, making sure to flip halfway through.
- When cooked to desired doneness, remove from the air fryer and rest for at least 5 mins.
- Top with refrigerated herb butter and serve.

Tips

- Pat your steak dry before rubbing on the olive oil. You're going to want to remove any of that excess moisture from the steak before adding the olive oil. This step is the most crucial when it comes to cooking a steak.
- Leave uncooked steak sit out for 20 mins. Add your salt to let some of the moisture of the steak get into that salt to help create the crust when cooked in the air fryer.
- Rest your steak after cooking. At least 5 mins but rest longer if you have the time.
- Make sure steaks do not touch in the air fryer to allow for consistent heat from the fan during the cooking process.
- You don't have to use the olive oil but it adds great flavor to your steaks.
- You can add any flavor or spices you'd like to your herb butter or your steak. Try seasoning your steak with Cajun, Creole or BBQ rubs. Or change up the herb butter to include rosemary, basil or tarragon.
- Note that the Herb Lemon Butter will serve 4-6 people.

Nutrition Info

Calories: 508.84kcal, Carbohydrates: 0.7g, Protein: 45.71g, Fat: 36.02g, Saturated Fat: 14.78g, Cholesterol: 137.86mg, Sodium: 121.08mg, Potassium: 638.92mg

Air Fryer Steak with Garlic-Herb Butter

Prep/Cook Time: 40 min, Servings: 2 servings

Ingredients

- One 1-pound sirloin steak, about 1 inch thick
- Kosher salt and freshly ground black pepper
- 4 tablespoons unsalted butter, at room temperature
- 1 tablespoon finely chopped fresh parsley
- 1 tablespoon finely chopped fresh chives
- 1 small clove garlic, finely grated
- 1/4 teaspoon crushed red pepper flakes

Instructions

- Allow the steak to sit at room temperature for 30 minutes before cooking.
- Preheat a 3.5-quart air fryer to 400 degrees F. Season the steak on both sides with a generous pinch of salt and several grinds of black pepper. Place the steak in the center of the air fryer basket and cook until desired doneness, about 10

minutes for medium-rare, 12 minutes for medium and 14 minutes for medium-well. Transfer the steak to a cutting board and allow to rest, about 10 minutes.

• Meanwhile, mash together the butter, parsley, chives, garlic and crushed red pepper in a small bowl until combined. Slice the steak against the grain into 1/4-inch-thick pieces. Top with the garlic-herb butter.

Nutrition Info

101 calories, 7g fat, 1mg cholesterol, 124mg sodium, 8g carbohydrate, 2g protein.

Jalapeno Lime Air Fryer Steak

Prep/Cook Time 45 mins, Servings: 4

Ingredients

• 1 lb flank steak *used flat iron – check keywords
• 1 lime juice and zest
• 1 jalapeno, sliced
• 3 cloves of garlic, minced
• 1/2 cup fresh cilantro, roughly chopped
• 2 tablespoons light brown sugar
• 1/2 teaspoon paprika
• 1/2 teaspoon fresh cracked pepper
• 1/4 cup avocado oil
• salt

Instructions

• Preheat the air fryer to 400F.
• Season the steak with salt and pepper. In a large mixing bowl, combine avocado oil, paprika, pepper, brown sugar, cilantro, garlic, jalapeño, and lime zest from 1 lime. Add the steak and toss to coat. Marinate for 30 minutes.
• Air fry for 10 minutes for medium rare, flipping the steak halfway through. When the steak is finished cooking, squeeze lime juice from half a lime over it. Allow it to rest with the air fryer lid open for 10 minutes before slicing. Serve the steak with steamed veggies, over a salad, or in a taco.

Oven Instructions

• To make the steak in the oven, preheat the broiler on high and cook for 6 minutes for medium rare. Squeeze lime juice from half a lime over the steak and allow it to rest for 10 minutes before slicing. Serve the steak with steamed veggies, over a salad, or in a taco.

Nutrition Info

Calories: 312kcal, Carbohydrates: 10g, Protein: 25g, Fat: 19g, Saturated Fat: 4g, Cholesterol: 68mg, Sodium: 64mg, Potassium: 432mg, Fiber: 1g, Sugar: 6g

Air Fryer Bone-in Ribeye Steak

Prep/Cook Time: 14 minutes

Ingredients

- 2-3 tablespoons butter softened
- 2 teaspoon freshly chopped parsley (dried works well too)
- 1 teaspoon chives
- 1 teaspoon thyme
- 1 (1.5-2 lb.) bone-in ribeye, preferably 1.5 inches in thickness
- Generous pinch of Kosher salt on both sides
- Freshly ground black pepper for both sides

Instructions

- In a small bowl, combine butter and herbs. Cover and refrigerate until hardened, about 15 minutes. You could make it prettier and roll in wax paper or plastic wrap to make a log.
- Season steak on both sides with salt and pepper.
- Place steak in the air fryer basket and cook at 375° for 12 to 16 minutes, depending on the thickness of the steak and how rare or done you wish you steak to be, flipping halfway through. I prefer medium-rare, so I flip mine at 7 minutes and do another 7 minutes on the other side.
- Top steak with a slice or two of herb butter to serve. Serve with vegetables or salad.

Nutrition Info

290 calories, 12 g fat (2 g saturated fat), 51 mg cholesterol, 380 mg sodium, 16 g carbohydrate, 3 g fiber, 31 g protein.

Air Fryer Steak Bites and Mushrooms

Prep/Cook Time: 50 mins, Servings: 4 servings

Ingredients

For the marinade:

- 1/2 cup soy sauce
- 1/4 cup olive oil
- 5 cloves garlic, grated
- 1 pinch salt
- 1 pinch pepper

For the steak and mushrooms:

- 1 lb sirloin steak, or ribeye, tri-tip, skirt steak, etc
- 227 grams whole mushroom, quartered
- 1 tbsp olive oil
- 1 pinch salt

Instructions

- Cut up your steak in 1 inch cubes and set aside.
- Combine the ingredients for your marinade and cover your steak bites with it and let it marinate in the fridge for 30 minutes.
- For the mushrooms, you can either marinate them alongside the steak or you can lightly toss them in olive oil with salt and pepper.
- Once ready, transfer the steak bites and mushrooms into your air fryer basket with a pair of tongs (Don't pour it into the basket as the liquid will just go through the basket).
- Set the airfryer to 400F for 10-12 minutes. Be sure to give the basket a shake at least twice.
- Once ready, serve alongside your carb of choice or store in an airtight container for up to 4 days as a meal prep.

Nutrition Info

Calories: 338kcal, Carbohydrates: 6g, Protein: 28g, Fat: 22g, Saturated Fat: 4g, Cholesterol: 69mg, Sodium: 1150mg, Potassium: 641mg, Fiber: 1g, Sugar: 2g

Lighten up Empanadas in an Air Fryer

Prep/Cook Time 45 Mins, Servings 2

Ingredients

- 1 tablespoon olive oil
- 3 ounces (85/15) lean ground beef
- 1/4 cup finely chopped white onion
- 3 ounces finely chopped cremini mushrooms
- 2 teaspoons finely chopped garlic
- 6 pitted green olives, chopped
- 1/4 teaspoon paprika
- 1/4 teaspoon ground cumin
- 1/8 teaspoon ground cinnamon
- 1/2 cup chopped tomatoes
- 8 square gyoza wrappers
- 1 large egg, lightly beaten

Instructions

- Heat oil in a medium skillet over medium-high. Add beef and onion; cook, stirring to crumble, until starting to brown, 3 minutes. Add mushrooms; cook, stirring occasionally, until mushrooms are starting to brown, 6 minutes. Add garlic, olives, paprika, cumin, and cinnamon; cook until mushrooms are very tender and have released most of their liquid, 3 minutes. Stir in tomatoes, and cook 1 minute, stirring occasionally. Transfer filling to a bowl, and let cool 5 minutes.
- Arrange 4 gyoza wrappers on work surface. Place about 1 1/2 tablespoons filling in center of each wrapper. Brush edges of wrappers with egg; fold wrappers over, pinching edges to seal. Repeat process with remaining wrappers and filling.
- Place 4 empanadas in single layer in air fryer basket, and cook at 400°F until nicely browned, 7 minutes. Repeat with remaining empanadas.

Nutrition Info

Calories 343, Fat 19g, Satfat 5g, Unsatfat 12g, Protein 17g, Carbohydrate 25g, Fiber 2g, Sugars 3g

Crispy Roast Pork Belly

Ingredients

- 0.8 – 1 kg pork belly
- 3 cups water
- 1 tsp sea salt,
- 1 tsp sugar

Skin Rub

- 1/2 tbsp vinegar
- 1 tsp sea salt

Meat Rub

- 1/4 tsp Chinese 5 spice powder
- 1/4 tsp sea salt

Instructions

- If there is any hair on the pork skin, scrape it off with a knife. Then wash the pork belly under a tap.
- In a fry pan on medium high, add the water, salt and sugar.
- Once boiling add the pork belly skin side down and cook for 8 minutes on each side.
- Once done, remove the pork belly and let it cool on a rack. Pat dry with some paper towel when it is cool enough to do so.
- Get a meat skewer and punch holes lots of holes into the skin of the pork belly – this usually takes me about 5 – 10 minutes. Do not punch holes so deep that it reaches the meat.
- Brush the pork skin with vinegar and then sprinkle half the salt. Let it rest for 10 minutes and repeat the process.
- Put the pork belly into the fridge uncovered and allow the skin to dry for a minimum of 12 hours. If you can, check on it every now and then to wipe off any moisture that comes to the surface.
- Take your pork belly out of the fridge and apply the meat rub on the sides and the bottom of the pork belly.
- Preheat your air fryer for 5 minutes then cook the pork belly for 40 minutes at 200 C (392 F).
- Once done, let it rest for 15 minutes before cutting.

Nutrition Info

49 calories, 1g fat (0 saturated fat), 2mg cholesterol, 157mg sodium, 9g carbohydrate (6g sugars, 2g fiber), 2g protein.

Air Fryer Pork Tenderloin

Ingredients

- brine ingredients (optional)
- 1.5 lb. pork tenderloin
- 1 Tbsp. olive oil
- 1/4 tsp. black pepper
- 1/4 tsp. garlic powder
- 1/4 tsp. salt (if not using a brine)

Instructions

- Brine the tenderloin according to brining instructions, optional.
- Take tenderloin out of fridge 20 minutes before cooking. Discard brine and rinse pork, if it was brined.
- Remove silver skin according to these instructions.
- Preheat air fryer to 400°F.
- In a small bowl combine olive oil, black pepper and garlic powder. If you did not brine the pork, then also add the salt. Stir.
- Rub olive oil mixture all over tenderloin.
- Place tenderloin in air fryer basket, bending it if needed for it to fit.
- Cook for 10 minutes. Flip.
- Cook until it has reached the desired doneness as indicated on an instant read thermometer, 145-160°F is recommended by the US Pork Board. This will take 8-15 more minutes.
- Let rest for at least 5 minutes before slicing into 1/2 to 3/4 inch slices. Serve immediately.

Nutrition Info

Calories Per Serving: 217, Total Fat 7.2g, Cholesterol 110.6mg, Sodium 235.6mg, Total Carbohydrate 0.3g, Sugars 0g, Protein 35.7g

Perfect Air Fryer Salmon

Prep/Cook Time 12 mins, Servings: 2 people

Ingredients

- 2 wild caught salmon fillets with comparable thickness, mine were 1-1/12-inches thick
- 2 tsps teaspoons avocado oil or olive oil
- 2 tsps paprika
- generously seasoned with salt and coarse black pepper
- lemon wedges

Instructions

- Remove any bones from your salmon if necessary and let fish sit on the counter for an hour. Rub each fillet with olive oil and season with paprika, salt and pepper.
- Place fillets in the basket of the air fryer. Set air fryer at 390 degrees for 7 minutes for 1-1/2-inch fillets.
- When timer goes off, open basket and check fillets with a fork to make sure they are done to your desired doneness.

Nutrition Info

Calories 288 Calories from Fat 170, Saturated Fat 2.6g, Cholesterol 78mg, Sodium 80.6mg, Potassium 52.5mg, Carbohydrates 1.4g, Fiber 0.8g, Protein 28.3g

Air Fryer Fish and Chips

Prep/Cook Time 20 mins

Ingredients

Fish and Chips ingredients

- 3-4 pieces cod or other white fish
- 1 cup all-purpose flour
- 2 eggs

- 1/4 tsp cajun seasoning or old bay
- salt and pepper to taste (cajun seasoning has salt already)

Instructions

Fish and chips instructions
- Beat two eggs in a bowl and set aside.
- Add flour to a second bowl and set aside.
- Add panko crumbs, and cajun seasoning, and set aside in a third bowl.
- Spray the air frying basket fairly liberally, and preheat air fryer to 400°f, 204°c for 5 minutes.
- Here is the process for coating the best air fryer fish ever. Coat fish in flour, then egg, then the panko mixture lastly, set the coated fish aside until all fish pieces are coated.
- Add the fish pieces to the air fryer, and cook at 400°f, 204°c for 10 minutes flipping the pieces with 5 minutes remaining.
- Since fish pieces vary in size and may affect cooking times, use a meat thermometer to make sure that your fish is cooked to a temperature of at least 145°f, 63°c.
- Plate and enjoy!

Nutrition Info

292 calories, 9g fat, 45mg cholesterol, 517mg sodium, 24g carbohydrate, 31g protein.

Frozen Fish in Air Fryer

Prep/Cook Time 17 minutes, Servings 4

Ingredients

- 4 fish fillets tilapia was used, frozen
- 1/2 tsp lemon pepper
- 1/2 tsp garlic powder
- 1/2 tsp onion powder
- 1/2 tsp salt
- 1 lemon
- parsley

Instructions

- Spray air fryer basket with non stick spray and lay frozen fillets inside, do not overlap them.
- Cut lemon in half, lightly squeeze some of one half on to fish and then sprinkle with seasonings. (if you are only doing 2 at a time then only add half of seasonings to top of first batch)
- Slice other half of lemon and put a thin slice of fresh lemon on each fillet.
- Close basket and set to 390 degrees for 12 minutes, then check. Timing will vary depending on how thick each piece is and how "done" you like your fish to be. Add 2 minutes at a time and check again if you want them to have more time.
- Sprinkle diced fresh parsley on top and serve.

Nutrition Info

Calories 12 Calories from Fat 9, Fat 1g, Saturated Fat 1g, Cholesterol 1mg, Sodium 292mg, Potassium 37mg, Carbohydrates 3g, Fiber 1g, Sugar 1g, Protein 1g

Crispy Air Fryer Cod

Prep/Cook 25 min

Ingredients

Fish

- 4 fresh cod fillets, 1" (2.5 cm) thick, (4–5 oz./125–150 g each)
- Oil for spraying
- ¼ cup (60 mL) mayonnaise
- 2 tbsp (30 mL) butter, melted
- ½ cup (125 mL) panko breadcrumbs
- ½ tsp (1 mL) Garlic & Herb Rub
- ¼ tsp (1 mL) salt
- ⅛ tsp (0.5 mL) black pepper

Roasted Vegetables

- ear corn, husk removed

- 8 oz. (225 g) asparagus (½ bunch), trimmed and sliced into 1–2" (2.5–5-cm) pieces
- 1 tsp (5 mL) olive oil
- ⅛ tsp (0.5 mL) salt

Herbed Lemon Vinaigrette

- 1 small lemon
- 2 tbsp (30 mL) olive oil
- 1 tsp (5 mL) Dijon mustard
- 1 tsp (5 mL) honey
- 1 tbsp (15 mL) chopped chives
- ⅛ tsp (0.5 mL) salt

Instructions

- Pat the cod fillets dry using a paper towel. Spray one cooking tray for the Deluxe Air Fryer with oil. Place the fillets on the cooking tray and brush each fillet with the mayonnaise using the Chef's Silicone Basting Brush.
- Mix the melted butter, panko, rub, salt, and pepper in a small bowl. Evenly divide the panko mixture onto the cod fillets, pressing firmly to adhere.
- For the roasted vegetables, remove the kernels from the cob with the Kernel Cutter. Add the corn, asparagus, olive oil, and salt to a medium bowl and stir to combine. Transfer vegetable mixture to the other cooking tray.
- Place the tray with the cod on the top rack and the tray with the vegetables on the bottom rack. Turn the wheel to select the ROAST setting; press the wheel to select. Turn the wheel to adjust the time to 9 minutes; press the wheel to start . Cook until the internal temperature reaches 140°F (60°C), adding more time if needed.
- For the vinaigrette, use the Citrus Press to juice the lemon into a small bowl. Add the remaining vinaigrette ingredients and whisk to combine.
- To serve, place the roasted vegetables on a serving platter. Spoon 1–2 tbsp (15–30 mL) of the vinaigrette on top of the vegetables. Carefully place the cod fillets on top of the vegetables and serve with remaining vinaigrette.

Nutrition Info

Calories 420, Total Fat 26 g, Saturated Fat 6 g, Cholesterol 80 mg, Sodium 630 mg, Carbohydrate 19 g, Fiber 1 g, Total Sugars 4 g (includes 1 g added sugars), Protein 29 g

Grilled fish fillet with pesto sauce

Ingredients

- 3 white fish fillets (200 g each)
- 1 tbsp olive oil
- pepper & salt
- 1 bunch fresh basil (15 g)
- 2 garlic cloves
- 2 tbsp pinenuts
- 1 tbsp grated parmesan cheese
- 1 cup extra virgin olive oil

Instructions

- Preheat the Airfryer to 320°F.
- Brush the fish fillets with the oil and season with pepper & salt. Place in the cooking basket of the Airfryer and slide the basket into the Airfryer. Set the timer for 8 minutes.
- Pick the basil leaves and place them with the garlic, pinenuts, parmesan cheese and olive oil in a food processor or pestle and mortar. Pulse or grind the mixture until it turns into a sauce. Add some salt to taste.
- Place the fish fillets on a serving plate and serve them drizzled with the pesto sauce.

Nutrition Info

321 calories, 5g fat (3g saturated fat), 75mg cholesterol, 366mg sodium, 2g carbohydrate (2g sugars, 0 fiber), 27g protein.

Air fryer potato-crusted fish fillets

Prep/Cook Time 28 min, Serves 4

Ingredients

- light mayonnaise
- ¼ cup(s) fresh parsley
- 1 Tbsp, chopped dill
- 1 Tbsp, chopped garlic powder

- ½ tsp table salt
- ¼ tsp black pepper
- ¼ tsp uncooked tilapia fillet(s)
- 1½ pound(s), 4 (6-oz) fillets
- dry potato flakes
- ¾ cup(s) cooking spray
- 5 spray(s)

Instructions

- Combine mayonnaise, parsley, dill, garlic powder, salt, and pepper. Pat tilapia fillets dry with paper towels. Pour potato flakes into a pie pan or rimmed plate.
- Preheat air fryer to 400°F. Spread 2 fillets with 1 Tbsp mayonnaise mixture each; dredge fillets in potato flakes, pressing gently to adhere. Spray air fryer with cooking spray. Arrange 2 coated fillets in air fryer and spray fillets with cooking spray. Air-fry until breading is crisp and fish is cooked through, about 10 minutes. Remove from air fryer and keep warm. Repeat process with remaining mayonnaise mixture, fillets, and potato flakes.
- Serving size: 1 fillet

Nutrition Info

86 calories, 228mg sodium, 12g carbohydrate (5g sugars, 4g fiber), 1g protein.

Air-Fryer Fish Cakes

Prep/Cook Time: 20 mins, Servings: 2

Ingredients

- Nonstick cooking spray
- 10 ounces finely chopped white fish (such as grouper, catfish or cod)
- ⅔ cup whole-wheat panko breadcrumbs
- 3 tablespoons finely chopped fresh cilantro
- 2 tablespoons Thai sweet chili sauce
- 2 tablespoons canola mayonnaise
- 1 large egg
- ⅛ teaspoon salt
- ¼ teaspoon ground pepper
- 2 lime wedges

Instructions

- Coat the basket of an air fryer with cooking spray.
- Combine fish, panko, cilantro, chili sauce, mayonnaise, egg, salt and pepper in a medium bowl; stir until well combined. Shape the mixture into four 3-inch-diameter cakes.
- Coat the cakes with cooking spray; place in the prepared basket. Cook at 400°F until the cakes are browned and their internal temperature reaches 140°F, 9 to 10 minutes. Serve with lime wedges.

Nutrition Info

399 calories; 16 g total fat; 2 g saturated fat; 150 mg cholesterol; 537 mg sodium. 731 mg potassium; 28 g carbohydrates; 3 g fiber; 10 g sugar; 35 g protein

Almond Crusted Fried Masala Fish

Prep/Cook Time: 50 minutes, Servings: Serves 4

Ingredients

- 2 pounds any firm while fish fillets, patted dry
- 4 tablespoons extra virgin olive oil
- 3/4 teaspoon turmeric
- 1 teaspoon cayenne pepper
- 1 teaspoon salt
- 1 tablespoon Fenugreek leaves
- 1 and 1/2 teaspoons freshly ground cumin
- 2 teaspoons amchoor powder or use lemon juice after air frying
- 2 tablespoons ground almonds (see note)
- To finish
- Extra lemon juice
- Chopped coriander leaves
- Sliced almonds

Instructions

- Set the fish aside in a mixing bowl.
- In a small bowl mix together the oil turmeric, cayenne, salt, fenugreek leaves, cumin and amchoor powder.
- Mix in the ground almonds.
- Pour the mixture over the fish and toss a few times to coat. Let the fish rest for 15 to 20 minutes.Press a few time to let the almonds and spices coat the fish.

- Place the fish in the air fryer basket. Cook for 10 minutes at 450 degrees. Turn and cook on the other side.
- Carefully remove the fish, sprinkle with extra lemon juice, chopped cilantro and a few sliced almonds.
- Serve as a snack or over rice as a meal.

Nutrition Info

274 calories, 10g fat, 63mg cholesterol, 457mg sodium, 16g carbohydrate, 28g protein.

Air Fryer Garlic Shrimp with Lemon

Prep/Cook Time25 mins, Servings: 2 -3 Servings

Ingredients

- 1 pound raw shrimp , peeled de-veined,
- Vegetable oil or spray , to coat shrimp
- 1/4 teaspoon garlic powder
- Salt , to taste
- Black pepper , to taste
- lemon wedges
- minced parsley and/or chili flakes (optional)

Instructions

- In a bowl add the shrimp, garlic powder, salt and pepper and toss to coat all of the shrimp evenly. Add shrimp to air fryer basket in a single layer.
- Air fry at 400°F for about 10-14 minutes, gently shaking and flipping halfway, depending on size of shrimp.
- Add the cooked shrimp to bowl, squeeze lemon juice on top. Sprinkle parsley and/or chili flakes and serve hot. So good!

Nutrition Info

Calories: 228kcal, Protein: 46g, Fat: 3g, Cholesterol: 571mg, Sodium: 1762mg, Potassium: 181mg

Easy Air Fryer Shrimp & Vegetables

Prep/Cook Time: 30 minutes, Servings: 3

Ingredients

- 1 pound thawed shrimp (about 21-25), peeled, deveined and tails removed
- 1 red bell pepper, cut into 1 inch chunks
- 1/2 yellow onion, cut into 1 inch chunks
- 1 tablespoon avocado oil or olive oil
- 1 teaspoon chili powder
- 1/2 teaspoon garlic powder
- 1/8 teaspoon cayenne pepper (a small pinch!)
- 1/2 teaspoon salt
- 1/2 teaspoon fresh ground black pepper
- optional to serve: rice, quinoa, pad thai noodles, more veggies, teriyaki sauce etc

Instructions

- Prep: Thaw and remove the tails from the shrimp. You can cook them tails on but I like to get it over with so I can enjoy my meal tail-free. Place the shrimp in a strainer to remove the excess liquid. If you're serving with rice, start that now. Make sure the veggies are prepped and ready to go.
- Mix it together: Add the shrimp, bell pepper, onion, oil, chili powder, garlic powder, cayenne pepper, salt & black pepper to a medium sized mixing bowl and stir to combine.
- Cook: Place seasoned shrimp and vegetable mixture into your air fryer basket. Set the air fryer to about 330F degrees (my air fryer is analog so its not exact). Air fry the shrimp and vegetables for 10-13 minutes total, shaking the basket halfway through.
- Serve: Serve with rice, quinoa, pad thai noodles, or any other carb you prefer. Store leftovers in an airtight container for up to 4 days.

Nutrition Info

Calories: 362 Fat: 7g Carbohydrates: 50g Fiber: 4g Protein: 43g

Air-Fryer Scallops

Prep/Prep/Cook Time: 25 min., 2 servings

Ingredients

- 1 large egg
- 1/3 cup mashed potato flakes
- 1/3 cup seasoned bread crumbs
- 1/8 teaspoon salt
- 1/8 teaspoon pepper
- 6 sea scallops (about 3/4 pound), patted dry
- 2 tablespoons all-purpose flour
- Butter-flavored cooking spray

Instructions

- Preheat air fryer to 400°. In a shallow bowl, lightly beat egg. In another bowl, toss potato flakes, bread crumbs, salt and pepper. In a third bowl, toss scallops with flour to coat lightly. Dip in egg, then in potato mixture, patting to adhere.
- Arrange scallops in a single layer on greased tray in air-fryer basket; spritz with cooking spray. Cook until golden brown, 3-4 minutes. Turn; spritz with cooking spray. Cook until breading is golden brown and scallops are firm and opaque, 3-4 minutes longer.

Nutrition Info

3 scallops: 298 calories, 5g fat (1g saturated fat), 134mg cholesterol, 1138mg sodium, 33g carbohydrate (2g sugars, 2g fiber), 28g protein.

Air Fryer Coconut Shrimp

Ingredients

For the shrimp

- 1/2 c. all-purpose flour

Kosher salt

- Freshly ground black pepper
- 1 c. panko bread crumbs
- 1/2 c. shredded sweetened coconut
- 2 large eggs, beaten
- 1 lb. large shrimp, peeled and deveined, tails on

For the dipping sauce

- 1/2 c. mayonnaise
- 1 tbsp. Sriracha
- 1 tbsp. Thai sweet chili sauce

Instructions

- In a shallow bowl, season flour with salt and pepper. In another shallow bowl, combine bread crumbs and coconut. Place eggs in a third shallow bowl.
- Working with one at a time, dip shrimp in flour, then eggs, then coconut mixture.
- Place shrimp in the basket of an air fryer and heat to 400°. Bake until shrimp is golden and cooked through, 10 to 12 minutes. Work in batches as necessary.
- In a small bowl, combine mayonnaise, Sriracha, and chili sauce. Serve shrimp with dipping sauce.

Nutrition Info

357 calories, 23g fat (9g saturated fat), 85mg cholesterol, 388mg sodium, 7g carbohydrate (4g sugars, 2g fiber), 31g protein.

Air Fryer Fried Shrimp

Ingredients

- 17-20 shrimp defrosted, we used jumbo, shells removed, deveined, tails attached
- 1 c bread crumbs Italian
- 1 tbsp taco seasoning
- 1 tbsp garlic salt
- 4 tbsp butter melted
- olive oil spray

Instructions

- Melt butter in a small bowl in microwave for about 30 seconds. Take shells off shrimp, devein them and pat dry with paper towels.
- In a bowl mix bread crumbs and seasonings. Preheat air fryer now for 5 minutes at 400 degrees.
- One at a time dip your shelled deveined jumbo shrimp into the butter, then into the bread crumb mixture. Use a spoon to completely cover the shrimp (keep tails out of mix). Carefully shake off excess crumbs and put into preheated air fryer.
- Fill basket with as many as possible without overlapping them. Spray all of them with olive oil spray.
- Close lid or push in basket and cook at 400 degrees for 5 minutes (for jumbo, smaller would not take as long). I did a round flipping them and one where I didn't. I think not flipping came out better as breading stayed in tact better.
- Enjoy immediately for best taste.

Nutrition Info

Calories 188 Calories from Fat 99, Fat 11g, Saturated Fat 6g, Potassium 59mg, Carbohydrates 16g, Fiber 1g, Sugar 1g, Protein 7g

Air Fryer, Easiest Breaded Shrimp

Prep/Cook Time: 30, Servings: 6 servings

Ingredients

- 1 pound of shrimp, peeled and deveined
- 2 eggs
- 1/2 cup of panko
- 1/2 cup of onion, peeled and diced
- 1 teaspoon of ginger
- 1 teaspoon of garlic powder
- 1 teaspoon of black pepper

Instructions

- Preheat your air fryer to 350 degrees.
- Then in one bowl, beat the eggs, in another bowl add the panko, onions, and spices
- Then dip the shrimp in the eggs, then the panko bowl
- Air fry for 5 minutes, then flip and then air fryer for another 5 minutes

Nutrition Info

309 calories, 9g fat (4g saturated fat), 54mg cholesterol, 498mg sodium, 29g carbohydrate (3g sugars, 5g fiber), 27g protein.

Crispy Batter Fried Shrimp

Ingredients

- 1 1/2 pounds large shrimp tails, peeled and deveined
- cooking oil of choice
- 1 cup almond flour
- 1/2 cup unsweetened almond milk
- 1 egg
- 1 teaspoon paprika
- 1 teaspoon garlic powder
- salt and pepper, to taste

Instructions

- Heat the oil of choice in a deep skillet over medium-high heat. Optionally, you can use an air fryer; preheat now if using.
- Clean and wash shrimp, leaving the tails intact.
- In a bowl, mix together the almond flour, egg, almond milk, garlic powder, paprika, salt, and pepper until combined.
- Once the oil is hot, hold the shrimp by the tail and dip into the batter and get a thick coating.
- Carefully place the shrimp into the oil, only cooking a few at a time to avoid overcrowding. Cook for 3-5 minutes, until golden brown on the outsides and opaque in the center.
- Repeat dipping and frying for all of the remaining shrimp. Service with your choice of dipping sauce, a fresh salad, or other low carb side. Enjoy!

Nutrition Info
Amount Per Serving: Calories: 350

Air Fryer Steak Bites & Mushrooms

Prep/Cook Time: 28 mins, Servings: 3 Servings

Ingredients

- 1 lb. steaks, cut into 1/2" cubes (ribeye, sirloin, tri-tip or what you prefer)
- 8 oz. mushrooms (cleaned, washed and halved)
- 2 Tablespoons Butter, melted (or olive oil)
- 1 teaspoon Worcestershire sauce
- 1/2 teaspoon garlic powder, optional
- flakey salt, to taste
- fresh cracked black pepper, to taste
- Minced parsley, garnish
- Melted butter, for finishing - optional
- Chili Flakes, for finishing - optional

Instructions

- Rinse and thoroughly pat dry the steak cubes. Combine the steak cubes and mushrooms. Coat with the melted butter and then season with Worcestershire sauce, optional garlic powder, and a generous seasoning of salt and pepper.
- Preheat the Air Fryer at 400°F for 4 minutes.
- Spread the steak and mushrooms in an even layer in the air fryer basket. Air fry at 400°F for 10-18 minutes, shaking and flipping and the steak and mushrooms 2 times through cooking process (time depends on your preferred doneness, thickness of the steak, size of air fryer).
- Check the steak to see how well done it is cooked. If you want the steak more done, add an extra 2-5 minutes of cooking time.
- Garnish with parsley and drizzle with optional melted butter and/or optional chili flakes. Season with additional salt & pepper if desired. Serve warm.

Nutrition Info

197 calories, 4 g fat (1 g saturated fat), 3 mg cholesterol, 593 mg sodium, 32 g carbohydrate, 2 g fiber, 10 g protein.

Air Fryer Jalapeno Poppers

Prep/Cook Time 22 minutes, Servings 18

Ingredients

- 10 jalapenos sliced in half lengthwise, seeds and membranes removed
- 10 slices bacon cut in half lengthwise
- 8 oz cream cheese room temperature
- 1 tsp cumin
- 1 c cheese Monterey jack
- olive oil spray

Instructions

- Spray air fryer basket with non stick spray.
- Mix together cream cheese, cumin and cheese in a bowl.
- Spoon cheese mixture into jalapenos that have been prepared as directed above.
- Wrap each jalapeno stuffed half with half a slice of bacon. Secure end with a toothpick
- Cook at 370 degrees for 6-8 minutes or until tops are golden brown.
- Remove, keep warm, and put another batch in. Serve with ranch dressing or other dipping sauces

Nutrition Info

Calories 122 Calories from Fat 99, Fat 11g, Saturated Fat 5g, Cholesterol 29mg, Sodium 161mg, Potassium 69mg, Carbohydrates 1g, Fiber 1g, Sugar 1g, Protein 4g

Air Fryer Cauliflower Munchies Recipe

Prep/Cook Time 35 minutes, 4 servings

Ingredients

- 1lb cauliflower florets
- 2 tablespoons avocado oil
- 1 tablespoon Everyday Seasoning
- 2 teaspoons cumin
- 2 teaspoons chile powder

- sea salt & pepper

Quick Chipotle Mayo sauce

- 1/2 cup reduced fat safflower mayo (or lower calorie mayo)
- 3 tablespoons sauce from chipotle peppers in adobo
- juice from 1 lime to taste

Instructions

- Set air fryer to 400F.
- In a large bowl, add oil and toss cauliflower in the seasoning.
- Arrange the cauliflower in the air fryer and air fry for 25 – 30 minutes, shaking the basket halfway through for best results.
- In another bowl, mix together the ingredients for the sauce.
- Add a pinch of sea salt & pepper to the cauliflower and enjoy with the dipping sauce.
- Air Fried Tex Mex Cauliflower Munchies

Nutrition Info

Calories 190, Protein 3g, Fat 16g, Carbs 11g, Fiber 4g, Sugar 4g

Crispy Veg Nuggets

Prep/Cook Time: 20 minutes, Servings: 4

Ingredients

- 200 gm Potatoes boiled and mashed
- 100 gm Broccoli grated
- 100 gm Peas crushed
- 70 gm Soy nuggets TVP soaked and crushed
- 1 cup Bread crumbs
- 50 gm Cheddar cheese
- 3 tbsp Coriander leaves chopped
- 3 tbsp Walnuts chopped
- 1 Green chillis chopped
- 1 tsp Salt to taste
- 1 tsp Black pepper powder

- 1 tbsp Italian Mixed herbs seasoning
- 1 tbsp Oil for brushing

Instructions

- In a large mixing bowl add boiled potatoes, grated broccoli, crushed peas, crushed and soaked soya nuggets, bread crumbs, coriander leaves, green chillies, walnuts, salt pepper and mixed herbs seasoning.
- Mix them and combine them well using your hands and make a soft dough.
- Now take a small portion of veg nugget mixture and shape it into square or round.
- Similarly make approximately 12 nuggets out of this total mixture.
- Brush the nuggets with oil.
- Preheat the air fryer at 150C for 3 minutes.
- Place these veggie nuggets in a single layer in air fryer basket and air fry at 200C for 7-8 minutes.
- Turn them over once in-between.
- Your air fried crispy veggie nuggets are ready.
- Serve them hot with tomato ketchup or hot chilli sauce.

Nutrition Info

Calories: 352kcal, Carbohydrates: 38g, Protein: 19g, Fat: 14g, Saturated Fat: 4g, Cholesterol: 13mg, Sodium: 910mg, Potassium: 445mg

Air Fryer Indian Bread Roll Recipe

Prep/Cook Time: 45 minutes, Servings: 6

Ingredients

- 4 medium-sized potatoes peeled and chopped
- 1/2 teaspoon salt
- water as needed

Spices for the stuffing

- 1 tbsp olive oil
- 1 teaspoon cumin seeds
- 1-2 Indian or Thai green chilies (Bird's eye) chopped

- 1 teaspoon coriander powder
- 1 teaspoon cumin powder
- 1/2 teaspoon turmeric powder
- salt as needed
- 1 teaspoon garam masala
- 1 tablespoon lime juice
- 1/4 cup chopped cilantro
- 12 slices white bread

Instructions

Boiling potatoes

- Place the peeled and chopped potatoes in the steel insert of the Instant Pot.
- Add water till the potatoes are submerged. Add 1/2 teaspoon of salt and mix well.
- Close the lid and set the vent to sealing position.
- Pressure cook on high for 8 minutes. When the cooking cycle is complete, release pressure by moving the vent to the venting position.
- Drain the water and mash the potatoes and transfer it into another bowl.
- Rinse the Instant Pot steel insert and wipe it clean.

Making the stuffing

- Add oil in the steel insert of the Instant Pot. Set the Instant Pot to 'Sauté' mode and adjust to normal.
- Once the oil is hot, add cumin seeds. When they start to sizzle, add green chilies. Sauté them for about 10 seconds.
- Add cumin and coriander powder along with salt, turmeric powder and garam masala. Mix well and then immediately add the potatoes along with lime juice and cilantro.
- Mash using either the back of your spatula or a potato masher until no lumps remain.

Making the rolls [Takes a minute per roll]

- Flatten the bread slices (one at a time) using a rolling pin.
- Take about 1.5 tablespoons of the potato stuffing and spread it evenly over a flattened bread slice.
- Roll the bread slices tightly into a long cylinder. Dab the edges of the bread with water to seal them.
- Repeat the process with the rest of the bread slices.

Air frying the rolls

- Set the air fryer at 400°F. Let it preheat for about 5 minutes.
- Place the rolls inside the basket and let it cook for about 10 minutes at 400°F. Note - depending on the size of your air fryer, 3 to 6 rolls might fit in and you'll have to make it in batches.
- Serve hot with green chutney or ketchup.

Nutrition Info

Calories: 244kcal, Carbohydrates: 44g, Protein: 8g, Fat: 4g, Saturated Fat: 1g, Sodium: 480mg, Potassium: 656mg, Fiber: 5g

Air Fryer Onion Pakoda (No Fry Tea Time Snack)

Prep/Cook Time 55 mins, Servings 3 peoople

Ingredients

- 2 cups Gram Flour or Besan 1 cup is 200 ml measurement
- 1 cup Sliced Onions I have used Red Onions
- 1/2 tsp Ajwain or Carom Seeds
- 1/4 tsp Hing or Asafoetida (skip this for gluten free recipe)
- 1 tsp Red Chilli Powder or Laal Mirch Powder
- 1/2 tsp Turmeric Powder or Haldi Powder
- 1/8 cup Rice Flour
- 1/2 cup Water for the batter
- 1 tsp Oil + As Required to Brush over the Pakodas in Air Fryer (it took me only 2 tblsp of oil for entire batch)
- Chopped Coriander Leaves as required
- Chopped Green Chillies as required
- salt to taste

Instructions

- Preheat the Air fryer at 200 degrees Celsius for 7 to 10 minutes
- In the meanwhile, take a bowl, add all the above ingredients such as flour, spices, coriander leaves, chillies, saltand mix everything well.
- Now add the water slowly and mix well until it forms a thick and sticky batter.
- Add 1 tsp of oil to this batter and mix well. This leads to crispy pakoras like the fried ones.

- Once the air fryer has been preheated, take small portions of the batter and place them on the Air fryer mesh.
- Brush the pakoras lightly with oil.
- Air fry them at 200 degrees Celsius for 10 minutes
- Flip the pakoras and lightly brush some oil, repeat the process for 7 minutes.
- You will find the edges crispy and the pakoras cooked well.
- Remove and serve hot.
- Repeat the process with the rest of the batter until you have a bowlful of pakoras to enjoy with a cup of tea or coffee

Nutrition Info

217 calories, 5g fat (0 saturated fat), 33mg cholesterol, 665mg sodium, 32g carbohydrate (10g sugars, 4g fiber), 14g protein.

Crispy Air Fryer Chickpeas

Total: 15 mins, Servings: 4 servingas

Ingredients

- 1 14-oz can chickpeas 425g
- 1 Tbsp olive oil 15 mL
- ½ tsp salt or seasoning of choice, see notes

Instructions

- Prep: Drain and pat chickpeas dry with a paper towel. Toss together with oil and salt (or your chosen seasoning).
- Cook: Spread in a single layer in your air fryer basket or rack. Cook at 390°F (200°C) for 8 to 10 minutes, or until crispy and lightly browned.

Nutrition Info

Calories: 183kcal, Carbohydrates: 27.1g, Protein: 5.9g, Fat: 6g, Saturated Fat: 0.8g, Cholesterol: 0mg

Roasted Okra

Ingredients

- 1/2 pound small whole okra , per person
- salt to taste
- pepper to taste (or seasonings of choice)
- olive oil spray (optional, if needed to prevent sticking)

Instructions

- First, start with the smallest okra you can find. Larger okra tends to be woody, which wouldn't work in this recipe.
- Wash the okra. Trim off any excess stems, but do not cut into the okra pod itself.
- Preheat the oven to 450 F. Spray a shallow baking dish with olive oil, if necessary, add okra, and season to taste. Give the okra one quick (1/2 second) spray with olive oil and put them into the oven. Bake, stirring every 5 minutes, until okra is browned on all sides, about 15 minutes. Serve hot out of the oven.

Air Fryer Instructions

- Preheat a standard air fryer to 390F or a Breville Air to 425F. Toss the freshly washed okra with seasoning and spread it in a single layer in the air fryer basket. Begin air frying, checking after about 7 minutes. Air fry until the okra is browning on all sides.

Nutrition Info

Calories 70 Calories from Fat 2, Fat 0.2g, Sodium 9mg, Carbohydrates 16g, Fiber 7g, Protein 5g

Prep/Cook Time: 10 mins, Servings: 4 servings

Ingredients

- 1 bunch kale about 5 cups, 8-10 oz
- 1 Tbsp olive oil 15 mL
- ¼ tsp salt
- Optional flavorings see notes

Instructions

- Prep: Wash and dry kale. Cut the leaves away from the spine, then roughly tear the leaves into bite-sized pieces. Massage oil into the leaves, making sure each piece of kale has a thin coat of oil. Sprinkle with salt and toss to coat.
- Transfer: Lay kale in a single layer in your air fryer basket, uncurling the leaves as much as possible while keeping them from overlapping too much (you may need to cook in batches).
- Cook: Air fry for 4 to 5 minutes at 375°F (190°C), shaking the pan once to help them cook evenly. Keep a close eye on them after 3 minutes. They're done when crispy!

NOTES

- Store kale chips in a paper bag, or in a loosely sealed plastic bag lined with a paper towel. They keep well at room temperature for up to a week. If they lose their crunch, throw them back in the air fryer for a minute or two.

Nutrition Info

Calories: 65kcal, Carbohydrates: 7.4g, Protein: 2.1g, Fat: 3.5g, Saturated Fat: 0.5g, Cholesterol: 0mg, Sodium: 178mg

Air Fryer Apple Chips

Ingredients

- 1-2 medium sized apples Red Delicious or Honeycrisp work best
- Cinnamon optional

Instructions

- Use a mandolin on the thinest setting (2.5mm) and slice the apples.
- Place apples in the air fryer basket. Sprinkle with cinnamon if using. Use a metal rack to cover the apple slices so they don't fly up into the fan while cooking.
- Cook on 300 degrees Fahrenheit for 16 minutes, flipping and rotating the apples every 5 minutes.
- After 16 minutes, remove the apples and allow them to cool for 5-10 minutes on a plate until they crisp up. Enjoy.

Notes

- The apples will still feel flexible after the 16 minute cook time. They will crisp up once they cool down. I usually stick to one apple for this recipe in order not to overlap my apple slices too much. I've also done it with two smaller sized apples.
- The apple chips can be stored in an airtight container. However, they are usually gone as soon as they are cooled. They are pretty addictive.
- Store or eat the apple chips as soon as they crisp up. If you leave them in the air for too long, they will soften again.

Nutrition Info

Calories: 95kcal, Carbohydrates: 25g, Protein: 1g, Fat: 1g, Saturated Fat: 1g, Sodium: 2mg, Potassium: 195mg, Fiber: 4g, Sugar: 19g

Air Fried Churros

Prep/Cook Time 23 mins, Servings 22 3-inch churros

Ingredients

- 3/4 cup plus 2 tbsp water
- 1/4 cup butter or 1/2 a stick
- 1 tbsp sugar
- a pinch of salt
- 3/4 cup flour
- 2 medium eggs

cinnamon sugar

- 1/2 cup sugar
- 1 tsp cinnamon

Instructions

- In a medium sauce pan, bring the water, butter, sugar and the pinch of salt to a boil over medium heat. Once the mixture boils, reduce the heat and add in the flour and mix rapidly using a wooden spatula. Continue stirring the mixture until the mixture thickens and does not stick to the sides of the pot.
- Transfer the mixture to a stand mixer bowl or heat proof bowl and mix using a paddle attachement. This will allow the churro dough to cool down so we can add the eggs. This process will take between 3-5 minutes.
- Once the churro dough is a little bit cooler add in the eggs one at a time while continuing to mix. The mixture will become a lot more sticky. At this point, transfer the churro mixture to a piping bag fitted with a star tip. I used the Wilton 1M
- On a parchment lined baking sheet pipe 3-4 inch long churros. Cut the end using a pair of scissors or knife. Place the baking sheet in the freezer for 30 minutes.
- 3 minutes before your churros are ready to be baked, preheat the air fryer to 360F. Gently remove the frozen churros from the parchment paper and place them into the air fryer basket and bake for 13-14 minutes. Depending on what air fryer you have you might have to bake these churros in multiple smaller batches. Place the leftover churros in the freezer so they don't get soft.

- In a shallow bowl or plastic bag combine the sugar and the cinnamon. Place the baked churros in the sugar mixture as soon as they come out of the air fryer, toss them in the cinnamon sugar mixture to coat them evenly.
- Serve with dulce de leche, sweetened condensed milk or even Nutella!

Nutrition Info

174 calories, 9g fat, 23mg cholesterol, 91mg sodium, 22g carbohydrate, 3g protein.

Air Fryer Apple Fritters

Prep/Cook Time 35 min, Servings 10

Ingredients

- 1/2 cup sugar
- 1/2 teaspoon ground cinnamon
- 1 cup chopped peeled apple (1 medium)
- 1 can (10.2 oz) Pillsbury™ Grands!™ Southern Homestyle refrigerated Buttermilk biscuits (5 biscuits)
- 3 tablespoons butter, melted

Instructions

- Cut two 8-inch rounds of cooking parchment paper. Place one round in bottom of air fryer basket. Spray with cooking spray.
- In small bowl, mix sugar and cinnamon. In another small bowl, mix chopped apple and 2 tablespoons of the cinnamon-sugar until well mixed.
- Separate dough into 5 biscuits; separate each biscuit into 2 layers. Press each into 4-inch round. Spoon 1 heaping tablespoonful of the apples into center of each round. Gently fold edges up and over filling; pinch to seal. Brush biscuits on all sides with 2 tablespoons of the melted butter.
- Place 5 of the biscuits, seam sides down, on parchment in air fryer basket. Spray both sides of the second parchment round with cooking spray. Top biscuits in basket with second parchment round, then top with remaining 5 biscuits.
- Set to 325°F; cook 8 minutes. Remove top parchment round; using tongs, carefully turn biscuits, and place in basket in single layer. Cook 4 to 6 minutes longer or until cooked through and apples are tender. Brush biscuits with remaining 1 tablespoon melted butter; roll in remaining cinnamon-sugar.

Nutrition Info
Calories 170, Calories from Fat 60, Total Fat 7g, Saturated Fat 4 1/2g, Protein 1g

Air Fryer Cheesecake Chimichangas

Ingredients

- 1 (8 ounce) brick of cream cheese, softened to room temperature
- 1/4 cup sour cream or plain nonfat greek yogurt
- 1-1/2 tablespoons granulated sugar
- 1 teaspoon vanilla extract
- 8 medium strawberries, quartered
- 1 medium banana, peeled and sliced
- 8 soft flour tortillas (8 inches - soft taco size)
- 8 teaspoons nutella
- olive oil spray
- 3 tablespoons melted butter
- cinnamon sugar (1 recipe)

Instructions

- In a medium mixing bowl, cream together the softened cream cheese, sour cream (or greek yogurt), sugar and vanilla until smooth.
- Divide the cream cheese mixture among 2 medium bowls and toss quartered strawberries in one and sliced bananas in the other. Gently stir to combine (or omit completely).
- Place a soft flour tortilla on to a clean work surface. Add 1/4 of the strawberry mixture to just left of center on the tortilla. Then add a teaspoon of nutella.
- Fold the left side of the tortilla over the filling. Fold the short ends in and roll like a burrito.
- Repeat this with the remaining strawberry mixture and then do the same with the banana mixture.
- Spray the chimichangas with olive oil spray and preheat your air fryer to 360°. Depending on the size of your air fryer, work in batches, placing the chimichangas seam-side down in and even layer and air frying for 8 to 10 minutes or until the tortilla is a deep golden brown.
- Once fried, place the chimichangas onto a wire rack set over a rimmed baking sheet. Brushe all sides, nooks and crannies with butter and then roll in a bowl of cinnamon sugar. Repeat.
- Prepare to fall in love.

Nutrition Info

Calories: 308, Total Fat: 14g, Saturated Fat: 7g, Trans Fat: 0g, Unsaturated Fat: 6g, Cholesterol: 20mg, Sodium: 292mg, Carbohydrates: 39g, Fiber: 3g, Sugar: 9g, Protein: 7g

Air Fryer Cake - Eggless & Vegan Cake

Prep/Cook Time 15 minutes, Servings: 4 Serving

Ingredients

- 1/4 Cup All-Purpose Flour
- 3 Tbsp Sugar *
- 2 Tbsp Cocoa Powder
- 1/8 Tsp Baking Soda
- 3 Tbsp Milk **
- 2 Tbsp Olive Oil
- 1 Tbsp Warm Water
- 2 Drops Vanilla Extract - optional
- Pinch of Salt
- 4 Raw Almonds (decoration) - thinly chopped - optional

Instructions

- Start by Pre-heating the Air Fryer for 2 minutes at 190C.
- In a medium bowl, add milk, oil, water, sugar and whisk to form a smooth batter. (I use a fork or a small whisk to mix everything).
- Now add baking soda, all-purpose flour, salt, cocoa powder to the wet mixture and whisk to form a smooth paste.
- Take an oiled/buttered 4inch cake pan (quiche pan) and pour the batter.
- Add chopped almonds on top.
- Place the baking pan in the preheated air fryer and air-fry for 10 minutes.
- Insert a toothpick to check if the cake is completely cooked (if need be air-fry for another minute).
- Remove the baking pan carefully from the air-fryer and let this cool completely.
- Once cooled, slice and enjoy.

Nutrition Info

Calories: 120, Total Fat: 8g, Saturated Fat: 1g, Trans Fat: 0g, Unsaturated Fat: 6g, Cholesterol: 1mg, Sodium: 78mg, Carbohydrates: 18g, Fiber: 1g, Sugar: 5g, Protein: 2g

Air Fryer Oreos

Ingredients

- 1 can Crescents Dough
- 8 Oreo cookies
- 1-2 tablespoons Powdered Sugar

Instructions

- Open the crescents and cover the Oreo cookies with the dough, making sure there are no air bubbles and it's completely covering the Oreo.
- Place the covered Oreos onto the air fryer rack and then cook in the air fryer at 350 degrees F for 4 minutes on the lower rack setting.
- Flip the Oreos once the tops are a light golden brown, about 3-4 minutes.
- Once the Oreos are done, dust them with powdered sugar before serving.

Nutrition Info

Calories: 159kcal, Carbohydrates: 21g, Protein: 2g, Fat: 8g, Saturated Fat: 3g, Sodium: 277mg, Potassium: 26mg, Fiber: 1g, Sugar: 9g

Air Fryer Cinnamon Sugar Dessert Fries

Prep/Cook Time 20 minutes, Servings: 4 Serving

Ingredients

- 2 sweet potatoes
- 1 tablespoon butter, melted
- 1 teaspoon butter, melted and separated from the above
- 2 tablespoons sugar
- 1/2 teaspoon cinnamon

Instructions

- Preheat your air fryer to 380 degrees.
- Peel and cut the sweet potatoes into skinny fries
- Coat fries with 1 tablespoon of butter.

- Cook fries in the preheated air fryer for 15-18 minutes. They can overlap, but should not fill your air fryer more than 1/2 full.
- Remove the sweet potato fries from the air fryer and place them in a bowl.
- Coat with the remaining butter and add in sugar and cinnamon. Mix to coat.
- Enjoy immediately.

Nutrition Info

Calories: 110, Total Fat: 4g, Saturated Fat: 2g, Trans Fat: 0g, Unsaturated Fat: 1g, Cholesterol: 10mg, Sodium: 51mg, Carbohydrates: 18g, Fiber: 2g, Sugar: 10g, Protein: 1g

5-Minute Air Fryer Sugar Doughnut Recipe

Prep/Cook Time 9 minutes, Servings: 8 Doughnuts

Ingredients

- 1 Can Large Pillsbury Biscuits
- 1/2 Cup Sugar
- 1/2 Tablespoon Cinnamon
- 5 Tablespoons Butter

Instructions

- Preheat air fryer to 330 degrees. To do this, simply turn your air fryer on at 330 degrees and let it run for about 3-5 minutes.
- In a medium bowl, mix together the cinnamon and sugar. Set aside.
- Open the can of biscuits and cut the center out of each one. (I use a small heart-shaped cookie cutter as my doughnut cutter is too small.)
- Place the larger, outside portion in your air fryer.
- Run for 4-7 minutes at 330 degrees. You may need to adjust this slightly depending on your particular air fryer model. After making this recipe in 3 different air fryers, I've learned it can take anywhere from 4-7 minutes to fully cook the doughnuts. The first time you make the recipe, you'll need to be sure to check to make sure they are fully cooked in the middle.
- As the doughnuts are cooking, melt the butter.
- Using a silicone pastry brush, coat the doughnuts with melted butter. Then lay in the bowl of cinnamon-sugar mixture and use a spoon to coat the top too.
- Gently shake off excess cinnamon sugar.
- Serve doughnuts hot.

- ***When you air fry the "holes", set your timer for just 2-4 minutes and top those with the butter and cinnamon/sugar too.

Nutrition Info

Calories: 135, Total Fat: 8g, Saturated Fat: 5g, Trans Fat: 1g, Unsaturated Fat: 3g, Cholesterol: 19mg, Sodium: 128mg, Carbohydrates: 16g, Fiber: 0g, Sugar: 13g, Protein: 1g

Pound Cake Bites with Bailey's Fudge Sauce

Prep/Cook Time: 55 minutes, Servings: 10

Ingredients

Bailey's Hot Fudge Sauce

- 2/3 cup heavy cream
- 1/2 cup Light Corn Syrup
- 1/3 cup brown sugar
- 1/4 cup cocoa powder
- 1/2 tsp salt
- 7 oz baking chocolate (semi sweet)
- 2 Tbsp butter
- 1 tsp vanilla extract
- 5 oz Bailey's Irish Cream
- 1 Pound Cake

Instructions

- Heat cream, corn syrup, sugar, cocoa powder, salt and 4 oz of chocolate over medium heat.
- Bring to a simmer, cook for 5 minutes, stirring constantly.
- Remove chocolate mixture from heat, add the rest of the chocolate, butter, vanilla extract and Irish Cream.
- Let cool for 20-30 minutes so it can thicken.
- Store in an airtight container in the fridge. When warming for use, heat for 25-30 seconds.
- While fudge sauce is cooling, cut the pound cake into 1.5" cubes. Put in air fryer and spray generously with oil.
- Cook in air fryer for 6 minutes on the first side, and 4-5 after turning them over, until cake is crispy and slightly crunchy.

- Pair the two together and dip, and eat!

Nutrition Info

Calories: 295, Total Fat: 14.4g, Saturated Fat: 9.4g, Cholesterol:31mg, Sodium: 113mg, Carbohydrates: 35.4g, Fiber: 1.3g, Sugar: 23.6g, Protein: 2.8g

Air Fryer Dessert Burritos

Prep/Cook Time: 12 minutes, Servings: 2

Ingredients

- 2 tortillas
- 2 tablespoon peanut butter
- 4 teaspoon chocolate chips
- 4 tablespoon mini marshmallows
- aluminum foil

Instructions

- Place tortilla on piece of foil.
- Spread peanut butter in the middle of the tortilla
- Sprinkle the chocolate chips and marshmallows on top
- Fold into a burrito and wrap foil around burrito.
- Repeat steps to make second burrito.
- Air fry at 400 degrees for 10 minutes.
- Carefully remove burritos and enjoy. NOTE: Burrito contents will be melted and extremely hot.

Nutrition Info

Calories: 328kcal, Carbohydrates: 49g, Protein: 7g, Fat: 12g, Saturated Fat: 4g, Cholesterol: 1mg, Sodium: 310mg, Potassium: 150mg, Fiber: 2g

Air-Fryer Chocolate Chip Cookie Bites

Prep/Cook Time: 30 mins, Servings: 17

Ingredients

- ½ cup butter, softened
- ½ cup packed brown sugar
- ¼ cup granulated sugar
- ½ teaspoon baking soda
- ½ teaspoon salt
- 1 egg
- 1 ½ teaspoons vanilla
- 1 ⅓ cups all-purpose flour
- 1 cup miniature semisweet chocolate pieces
- ⅓ cup finely chopped pecans, toasted

Instructions

- Cut a piece of parchment paper to fit in fryer basket. In a large bowl beat butter on medium to high 30 seconds. Add both sugars, baking soda, and salt. Beat on medium 2 minutes, scraping bowl occasionally. Beat in egg and vanilla until combined. Beat in as much of the flour as you can. Stir in any remaining flour. Stir in chocolate chips and pecans.
- Drop dough by measuring teaspoon onto parchment paper about 1 inch apart. Carefully transfer parchment paper to air fryer basket. Cook at 300°F for 8 minutes or until golden brown and set. Remove parchment to a wire rack to cool. Repeat with remaining cookie dough.

Nutrition Info

188 calories; 10 g total fat; 5 g saturated fat; 1 g polyunsaturated fat; 3 g monounsaturated fat; 25 mg cholesterol; 156 mg sodium. 71 mg potassium; 24 g carbohydrates; 1 g fiber; 15 g sugar; 2 g protein

CONCLUSION

The Smart Oven Air or Air Fryer has a lot of functions and is a lot bigger than the rest of the Breville ovens. It is also the most expensive Breville oven. So is the Smart Oven Air worth it? In our opinion, it all depends on whether you will actually use it. Breville packs a lot of features into their ovens and Air Fry is a great addition to them. Air frying is great for many people who want to cook healthier.

Lightning Source UK Ltd.
Milton Keynes UK
UKHW032040051022
410003UK00004B/314